Seven Paths

to Peace

ROTARY INTERNATIONAL

EVANSTON   ZURICH

Contents

Where the Paths Begin

THIS IS A BOOK largely about Rotarians and the "paths" they are traveling toward world peace. Rotarians have no monopoly on the paths to peace—nor would they say there are only seven. There are other paths to peace than those discussed within these pages, but Rotarians in the more than 50 years of existence of Rotary clubs have developed through discussion and action several concrete statements about, and approaches to, peace.

Rotarians—more than a half million of them—belong to Rotary clubs in more than 100 lands and, although each club is an autonomous body, they have what might be loosely termed a world-wide "understanding" about certain things. In convention assembled, Rotarians have agreed that specific words express what they generally believe. The board of directors, representing all Rotarians, also has taken concerted action about Rotary aims on peace —often on the recommendation of committees or other Rotarians.

Rotary's one object has four parts, or avenues:

To encourage and foster the ideal of service as a basis of worthy enterprise and, in particular, to encourage and foster:

First. The development of acquaintance as an opportunity for service;

Second. High ethical standards in business and profession; the recognition of the worthiness of all useful occupations; and the dignifying by each Rotarian of his occupation as an opportunity to serve society;

Third. The application of the ideal of service by every Rotarian to his personal, business, and community life;

Fourth. The advancement of international understanding, good will, and peace through a world fellowship of business and professional men united in the ideal of service.

Paragraph four is called "the avenue of international service," but paragraph one implements the genius of Rotary in international service. "The development of acquaintance as an opportunity for service" pinpoints the essential—*how?* There, at the simple heart of Rotary, is the impulse that brought together Paul Harris and his friends in Chicago in 1905. Acquaintance is Rotary's special gift for the advancement of understanding, good will, and peace—and the simple formula of Rotary's success in overcoming the isolation of men from each other. Acquaintance relaxes tensions in business, creates the kindling spark of selfless contribution to the community, and becomes the basic solvent which Rotary offers for problems which separate and divide mankind.

If the foregoing seems elementary to the experienced Rotarian, it should be said that non-Rotarians also have an abiding interest in what Rotarians have done, and are doing, to create conditions in which peace can exist. Historically, Rotarians have shared their international insights and have not hesitated to be a leavening influence. This book is addressed to non-Rotarians, too.

Rotary International is an association of autonomous Rotary clubs, not a body which takes corporate action. It embraces no causes except the object of Rotary and specific policies and projects which implement that object.

Impelled by the vision of, and the frightening necessity for, peace based on world fellowship, Rotarians have explored the techniques of building understanding among men of differing nations, creeds, and colors. They have also developed, in co-operation with others, an Outline of Policy in international service which has been adopted by the board of directors of Rotary International. Since the purpose of this book is to develop seven facets of this Policy *as they apply to the individual Rotarian*, additional background is appropriate.

This Policy is the product of painstaking research, the result of a questionnaire addressed to Rotarians throughout the world. Rotarians, distinguished by their interest in international service, were asked to examine their feelings and to describe their attitudes toward *world* affairs. The objective was to assemble a composite statement applicable to men of all nations concerning what it means to have the international outlook of a Rotarian.

Replies to the questionnaire reflected many, and differing, aspects of rich experience. Even to the internationally-minded, things do not look the same when seen from a village in the Andes, from the heart of an empire, or from a teeming city of Asia. Many hours were spent by committees of Rotary International in comparing and correlating a consensus that could be phrased in a brief but comprehensive statement.

The resulting statement reveals international service as an assertion of the sovereignty of the human spirit. This Policy connotes action. It is addressed to the articulate and the informed and the compassionate—not to the apathetic and unconcerned:

The Responsibility of the Individual Rotarian

Each Rotarian is expected to make his individual contribution to the achievement of the ideal inherent in the fourth avenue of service.

Each Rotarian is expected to so order his daily personal life and business and professional activities that he will be a loyal and serving citizen of his own country.

Each Rotarian wherever located, working as an individual, should help to create a well-informed public opinion. Such opinion will inevitably affect governmental policies concerned with the advancement of international understanding and good will toward all peoples . . .

This is only the beginning of the Outline of Policy in international service, but it clearly points to the individual Rotarian—wherever he may be. Then, there follows an analysis of the directions in which each Rotarian will exert his leadership. Seven paths, in effect, are commended by the experience of Rotarians from far and wide. The value of self-examination is aided by the companionship of many searching minds. There is no pretense of finality. The statement is intended as a springboard—a challenge to independent thinking.

Could you choose these paths as your own and follow them in the course of service they prescribe?

A decision of such personal importance cannot be undertaken lightly. Little is gained by one who reads through the statement, wags his head approvingly or rejects it out of hand or appraises it like the curate did his famous egg, as "good in parts." Read in this casual manner, the statement can be easily dismissed.

Accordingly, the remainder of the statement on "The Responsibilities of the Individual Rotarian" is not quoted at this point. Instead, each of the following seven chapters deals with a part of it. Each chapter opens with the pertinent section. One by one, each of the seven paths is scrutinized in the context of prevailing conditions, problems, and opportunities for service to which it leads. The concluding chapter, entitled "Impact," chronicles examples of the impact of Rotary—each example another direction-sign along the paths leading to peace among men.

If Rotarians and others are attracted to these paths in increasing numbers, it could make a vast difference in the vitality and impact of Rotary. More important, however, is the possibility that all humanity might somehow avert the calamity of war and the destruction of civilization itself. This is why Rotarians believe that if there is failure in the avenue of international service, there may be no need for concern about the other avenues of service.

The present dilemma of mankind can be compared to the situation in which the crew of the *Kon-Tiki* found itself on 7 August, 1947. On that day the westward current, which had carried the balsa-log raft and its six-man crew 4,300 miles across the Pacific, thrust the tiny raft closer and closer to the threatening Raroia Reef. A north wind diverted the raft for a while, but the coral reefs still "lay in ambush." Then the wind died away, and slowly, but inexorably, the raft drifted toward the coral wall. The rhythm of the sea changed, rising to an angry pitch which boiled and seethed to a foaming, writhing climax at the reef. The surf, first a dull drone, became as sharp as a drum roll, as the *Kon-Tiki* was dragged toward the reef.

Beyond the surf line the crew could see islands with palm trees behind a calm lagoon. But there could be no thoughts of idyllic islands as the raft plunged toward the reef. The crew had not the manpower to resist the tide.

If the raft disintegrated, the crew would surely be cut to death by the coral. If the raft held, they might live to swim the peaceful lagoon. If the tide perchance lifted the raft clear of the reef, they might live to tell their story.

The allegory is clear. Mankind has brought civilization a long and difficult distance, suddenly to find it threatened by total annihilation—hydrogen war. The drift toward war is unmistakable, whether it should come this year, next year, ten years from now, or whenever. The reefs are rugged and frightening. Is there a way around them—a course which is yet to be discovered? Are there sufficient hands to reverse the drift toward destruction?

Yes, there is a way, and this book is presented in the hope and belief that there are thousands of hands which up to now have not been lifted—but which now may be persuaded to row a new and firm course.

1

The Path of Patriotism

He will look beyond national patriotism and consider himself as sharing responsibility for the advancement of international understanding, good will, and peace.

He will resist any tendency to act in terms of national or racial superiority. *

A PROFESSOR of Princeton University recalls his brief acquaintance with a sailor in San Francisco—a boy on his way home to Chicago after long service in the Pacific area. The magic of the city of the Golden Gate apparently made no impression on him. Asked why he did not like San Francisco, he pondered the question for a moment and then replied with conviction: "Well, this here town isn't Chicago."

* From the Outline of Policy in International Service.

"In a flash," the professor remarks, "I felt that I understood more of the nature of nationalism than many a learned tome had ever taught me."

> Breathes there the man with soul so dead
> Who never to himself has said:
> 'This is my own, my native land.'
> Whose heart hath ne'er within him burned
> As home his footsteps he hath turned
> From wandering on a foreign strand?
> If such there breathe, go, mark him well
> For him no minstrel raptures swell:
> High though his titles, proud his name,
> Boundless his wealth as wish can claim—
> Despite those titles, power and pelf,
> The wretch, concentred all in self,
> Living shall forfeit fair renown,
> And doubly dying shall go down
> To the vile dust from whence he sprung,
> Unwept, unhonour'd, and unsung.

These unforgettable lines of Sir Walter Scott provide emotional overtones for that part of the Outline of Policy which states the premise for international service: *Each Rotarian is expected to be . . . a loyal and serving citizen of his own country.* It is taken for granted as a natural extension of the motto, "Service Above Self."

Nationalism, often indicted for narrowness, is not really narrow in origin; in essence it is an expansive, generous attitude of which only "the wretch concentred all in self" is incapable. One Rotarian speaking at a convention of Rotary International recalled the Latin proverb: *Dulce et decorum est pro patria mori* (how sweet and seemly it is to die for the fatherland) and continued:

It takes a high order of patriotism to make a man willing to die for his country, but it takes an even higher order of patriotism to make a man willing to die, if need be, to make his country right when his country is wrong. Then patriotism, when it comes to its very climax, is that patriotism we find in one of Rotary's principles where it talks about international good will and understanding, where it gets big enough to leap across national boundaries and encompass all humanity.

Looking back over man's journey through the ages, this same impulse to leap over local barriers is discovered from age to age. As he crept into the shelter of a tribal cave, the primitive savage foreshadowed the dictum of the philosopher Hobbes that "the life of man without society is poor, mean, nasty, brutish, and short." When tribes resisting an invader submitted to a common order of battle, the seeds of a larger relationship were planted. Later, there were moats, bridges, and walls to hold the communities *inside*—and the intruders *outside*. With growth of communication and expanding horizons of men's interests and enterprises, cities and states began to merge into nations.

The process is vividly personalized in Bernard Shaw's play, *Saint Joan*, where the Earl of Warwick and the Bishop of Beauvais are discussing the Maid's appeal as a menace to their feudal interests. They marvel that a simple peasant girl could look beyond her farm and village to conceive of France as her country. Yet indeed she did, and her countrymen rallied eagerly to her vision. "The old order changes, giving place to new." Normans, Bretons, Gascons, and the rest emerge as Frenchmen devoted to homeland.

Similarly, a "new order" was articulated by a Japanese student who wrote the winning essay in an international understanding and good will contest sponsored by a Rotary club. She wrote:

> Each country has its own peculiar way of life, cultivated through her long history and acclimatized to her natural circumstance; to such a way of life only one principle can not be applied. As the proverb says, 'Every man in his humor,' each country is destined to have its own special character . . . It is absolutely necessary for all countries to understand each other's character so as to promote mutual friendship and good will, before running the risk of opposition or strife . . . .
>
> Individual fundamental human rights must be respected, even if someone has a different idea from ours—because he is Man. In the same way, the sovereignty of a country must reasonably be respected, no matter how different her way of life may be. To expect the prosperity and welfare of one's country alone—disregarding the happiness of others— is wrong . . . Only when we build up a firm, true friendship based on the generous approval of others, can we hope for the eternal peace of the world . . . .

The path of patriotism, far from embarrassing the Rotarian, is proposed to him as the basis of international service. It leads to wider acquaintance, based on respect and mutual esteem. In the mind of the Rotarian there is no more contradiction between patriotism and international-mindedness than there is between being a good father of his family and being a worthy citizen of his community. Can the one, in fact, be accomplished without the other?

A contradiction does exist, however, in some minds. Perhaps the study of history, which Gibbon called "the register of the crimes, follies, and misfortunes of mankind," contributes to this feeling. There is a kind of patriotism which is nourished by grievances and fears, which exists mostly to foment hatred and hysteria for selfish ends, and which becomes, in the words of Doctor Johnson, "the last resort of scoundrels."

The best defense against this kind of patriotism is a more careful examination of national pride and of the directions toward which it leads. Would not the people of your country—any country—be happier and safer if the foe of today were transformed into a friend? It can happen. It is happening, and it has happened repeatedly throughout history. For centuries the French and the English were at daggers drawn. They disputed the supremacy of Europe in bitter warfare—on the continent and over the seven seas from the wildernesses of America to the steaming swamps of India. Later, they became friends. To the embattled patriots of bygone days this friendship might be incredible treason, yet both countries have benefited in security and prosperity. Much of the progress of the great nineteenth century became possible when the enmity between England and France was laid to rest.

Probing even deeper, do we love our country because of the hatred and fear she evokes in men of other nations? Or, is not that hostility a source of shame and sorrow? Do we not glory in our country's contribution to the spiritual, cultural, and material progress of mankind? And is not the true patriot the person who enlarges the glory of his land by projecting his service beyond its boundaries?

Through much analysis, the true patriot builds a strong defense. Looking beyond national patriotism, as suggested in the Outline of Policy, true patriotism justifies itself. Yet, in the process of self-justification there is danger. In the Outline, a warning immediately follows: *He will resist any tendency to act in terms of national or racial superiority.*

11

Now, the tables are turned. The critic is no longer out-side in the person of the chauvinist. Now the enemy is seen as coming from *within*—from the human tendency to seek superiority. It is not easy to resist, so desperately we want to be right. And it is difficult to be right without being self-righteous.

A Chinese Rotarian illustrated the harm done to inter-national relations by thoughtless, prideful assertions of superiority—among his own people along with the rest. He called it one of the major factors holding back the advance of civilization, the secret weapon of those who would divide in order to enslave.

The following letter, written in 1793 and sent from the emperor of China, Ch'ien Lung, to King George III of England, illustrates an ages-old, universal problem:

"You, O King, live beyond the confines of many seas; never-theless, impelled by your humble desire to partake of the benefits of our civilization, you have despatched a mission respectfully bearing your memorial. . . . I have perused your memorial; the earnest terms in which it is couched reveal a respectful humility . . . which is praiseworthy. . . .

If you assert that your reverence for our Celestial Dynasty fills you with desire to acquire our civilization, our cere-monies and code of laws differ so completely from your own that, even if your envoy were able to acquire the rudi-ments of our civilization, you could not possibly transport our manners and customs to your alien soil. . . .

"Swaying the wide world, I have but one aim in view, namely, to maintain a perfect governance and to fulfill the duties of the state. Strange and costly objects do not inter-est me. If I have commanded that the tribute offerings sent by you, O King, are to be accepted, this was solely in con-sideration for the spirit which prompted you to despatch

them from afar. Our Dynasty's majestic virtue has pene-
trated into every country under Heaven, and kings of all
nations have offered their costly tribute by land and sea.
As your ambassador can see for himself, we possess all
things. . . ."

Yet, within our own persons we carry around this tendency to trumpet our superiority. It is often seen in tourists
and those who live abroad, in the reception of immigrants,
or in the treatment of persons of another race. Brutal assertions of national or racial superiority are no more bit-
terly remembered than half-conscious gestures of conde-
scension. They are entered into the record of wrath that
poisons international relations.

A Rotarian and his wife from Texas, U.S.A., were traveling in France and stopped at a small village inn for the
night. The lady at the registration desk must have heard
of Texas, for she smiled knowingly at the wide-brimmed
hat worn by the man. When she heard him say, "My wife
and I would like a room for the night," she reddened and
stammered a little.

"You do have rooms, don't you?" the man asked.

"*Oui, monsieur,* we have rooms, but they are not what
you Americans say—*moderne*. They are not the best, *monsieur*."

"Madam," said the man from Texas, "where we come
from all you need is a blanket and a pile of hay. We'll be
glad to stay with you."

Of such is the record of personal humility and respect
which brightens international relations.

We may be helped toward the path of genuine patriotism by reminding ourselves that, personally, we have
added little to the store of our national or racial greatness,

and that individually many persons of other nations and races surpass us in accomplishment. What *is* within our power is a willingness to serve through developing acquaintance with them.

Rotarians enjoy special privileges in the field of acquaintance; over the world, to cite one example, there are many Rotary clubs with different nationalities represented in their membership. Many clubs claim a score or more whose harmonious co-operation is regarded as an important service to the community, to say nothing of its broader implications for mankind. As conceived by one pioneer of Rotary:

> If Rotary had been especially constructed to serve only in this capacity, it could not be a more perfect machine. It shocks no faith, for all religions are equally welcome within its portals. There are no secrets, no mysterious rites to raise doubts in the minds of non-Rotarians. And then, most happily, its great objective is simplicity itself, understandable to all men. What a splendid banner to emblazon to a suffering world.

It should be clearly understood, however, that the abolition of national, religious, and cultural differences is not a part of the Rotary program. On the contrary, the diversity of human expression is regarded as a matter for rejoicing, and never as a barrier to understanding and co-operation. In a world which is shrinking with each jet-propelled second, how dull it would be if this earth's glorious variety were reduced to drab uniformity. Much of the pleasure—and yes, the fun—of international service is in discovery and appreciation of these cherished differences.

This is not to minimize the problems created by differences, for Rotarians in more than 100 countries and geographical regions have special reason for being aware of these problems. From the Union of South Africa comes a story of Rotary action in the face of differences and of danger, too. On the Wednesday following serious riots in neighboring towns, the Rotary club had arranged to sponsor a concert given by the prize-winners of a Bantu music festival. One of the trophies to be awarded was a gift from a Rotarian in the British Isles but, under the circumstances, the question was raised whether Rotarians should attend the concert with their wives.

Upon reflection, however, club members took heart from the progress which had been achieved locally in race relations through African ward elections, sporting clubs, and a determined attack upon housing problems. Rotarians turned out in force, with their families, for the concert.

This step was amply rewarded. In his closing speech the African chairman asked his largely African audience:

> What is this Rotary movement, and how is it that a Rotarian from Great Britain has sent us a cup? These Rotarians believe that they must work for better race relations all over the world, and we Africans have seen with our own eyes how this group of Europeans is living up to this belief. We Africans must help these men with their work. We are progressing without violence. We do not need violence.

Progressing without violence. Could there be a more patriotic wish by any man of any country?

The path of patriotism is one path to peace; it offers opportunities for tangible, personal service by Rotarians in all countries. Incidents occur every day which challenge the true patriot to declare his interpretation of nationalism as a generous and expansive way of life. For him, national holidays are not occasions of vainglorious boasting but reminders of his responsibility to help build respect for all peoples. He will use all the vehicles of acquaintance available to Rotarians in creating friendships with people of all nations and races, for therein lies the hope and glory of his own beloved land.

2

The Path of Conciliation

He will seek and develop common grounds for agreement with peoples of other lands.

A SECRETARY of state for external affairs of Canada relayed to the Golden Anniversary convention of Rotary International this report of a visit to the Afghanistan frontier:

> When we got there, we found a chain across the middle of the road. On one side of the chain was an Afghan sentry and on the other a Pakistan sentry. The Afghan sentry was armed to the teeth. I was not quite sure what would happen if I crossed the frontier. So, standing firmly on Pakistan territory, I held out my hand to the Afghan sentry and smiled. He rested his rifle on a rock, broke into a broad grin, and invited me to step over the chain. I did this and shook him warmly by the hand.

> Rotary invites and assists all men to step over the chain of national prejudice, national pride, and shake each other

° From the Outline of Policy in International Service.

warmly by the hand—so, may it grow and flourish and prosper in this great work.

Smiles and handshakes are universal passports to understanding. They relax tensions and create an atmosphere in which conciliation of disputes becomes possible. Of themselves, however, they do not resolve conflicts. Thinking persons ask themselves in desperate sincerity, how can nations committed to different systems of life and government be persuaded to fulfill their aspirations without recourse to violence?

A fable discloses the root of several obstacles to conciliation. It tells of an angel who appeared at a high level conference of great powers. The angel announced that Heaven was much distressed by their disagreements. "The trouble," said the angel, "is that each of you can veto what the others want. I am instructed to grant one wish to each of you—a wish that the others cannot prevent being carried out."

One representative responded quickly: "I wish that a tidal wave would engulf your whole country."

"Well!" exclaimed the next diplomat, "if you want to play rough, I wish that a great plague would descend upon you and kill off all your people."

There was a pause, and the celestial visitor turned to the third delegate. "All I want," said he, mildly, "is a good cup of tea, but take care of the other two gentlemen first."

Does not this fable reflect the basis on which nations large and small approach the process of conciliation? Without wishing the physical extermination of the other party, there is the tacit assumption that he must surrender his purposes and principles—otherwise, agreement is impossible. For all practical purposes this attitude assumes a

18

world in which each nation can "go it alone," if necessary, and overcome its difficulties with other nations simply by ignoring them.

He will seek common grounds of agreement with peoples of other lands. The expectation is not implied here that any nation will transform itself into the image of another. The objective is a cool and dispassionate examination of actual conditions, needs, and aspirations of the peoples concerned. Neither side is expected to concede its principles or purposes in the agreement; instead, each seeks confirmation of its goals in the benefits resulting from co-operation. This attitude assumes that other nations—far from being external entities which can be ignored—are people like ourselves and that, because of this likeness, agreements, solutions, and settlements can be found or created which will be beneficial to all concerned.

Too idealistic? Not at all. History abounds with instances that testify to the realism of this approach. For centuries Moslems and Christians battled for supremacy. Neither group has abandoned its goal, but conflict has been replaced generally by a mutual forbearance in the pursuit of other interests. Russia and Britain engaged in a prolonged cold war throughout the nineteenth century, but the first and second world wars found them acting as allies. The belligerents of the second world war have become, in several cases, close friends.

The approach taken by belligerents has something to do with results, too. Two neighbors quarreled over the placement of a line fence. Finally, one of them, weary of bitter conflict, sold his property. After the sale, he explained the problem to the new owner. "You will have trouble with your neighbor," he said. "He thinks the line fence should be five feet over on your land. Be prepared to go to court with him."

The new owner moved in. Immediately, the neighbor approached him with fire in his eyes. "You will have to move that fence," he warned. "It's five feet too far on my land. I'll take you to court to prove it."

"That won't be necessary," the new owner said. "I've heard about your complaint, so you move the fence where you think it should go—and that will be fine with me."

The neighbor wilted with unbelief and went away muttering incoherently. The fence was never moved.

Rotarians have demonstrated the validity of this attitude in numerous settings of tension. Perhaps the most remarkable was a boundary dispute between Ecuador and Peru which had gone unsettled for 150 years and had caused three wars. At a crucial moment Rotarians of both countries persuaded their governments to permit an attempt at conciliation. Three Rotarians appointed by the president of Rotary International met in a neutral country, and in four-and-a-half days they devised a solution which was later adopted by a conference of the inter-American organization.

War in the Chaco came to an end, partly as a result of efforts by Rotarians in the belligerent countries and in Chile. Fierce tensions on the borders of Uruguay and Brazil were relaxed through the influence of Rotarians of the two countries who lived near the frontier. More recently, Rotarians of Costa Rica and Nicaragua helped to prevent conflict between their countries by a campaign of friendly visits and correspondence with non-Rotarians.

The anguish produced by the partition of India and Pakistan will be long remembered. Hordes of homeless refugees roamed the lands. Anarchy threatened. Restoration of order was attributed largely to the actions of individuals—many of whom were Rotarians. As one of the few organizations where Hindus and Moslems met socially, Rotary clubs formed conciliation committees which "sent into the streets patrols consisting of leading Moslems and Hindus. They addressed meetings and called upon the people to abate their inflammatory attitude and to resolve their common difficulties."

Most Rotarians, however, do not have opportunities to follow the path of conciliation in such dramatic circumstances. They can, however, seek common grounds for agreement through personal acquaintance and discussion with other Rotarians—both with Rotarians in their own clubs and in clubs in distant places. In these ways any Rotarian can use Rotary facilities for exploring with men of good will the real needs and aspirations of their countrymen. Having discovered what interests are vital, the search for means of satisfying them without prejudice to the vital interests of other nations can be undertaken. Meanwhile, the fresh insights and the constructive quest for agreement can be shared with the people of the community.

It is apparent, then, that those who would follow the path of conciliation must possess imagination and ingenuity. One must have the temerity to imagine himself as a sort of foreign minister vested with responsibility for the international relations of his country, but free from the pressures which surround foreign ministers. The challenge is to consider every international problem on its merits, in _all_ its aspects. Can you see a solution which you could recommend to your fellow citizens?

Actually, this projection of ourselves into such a role

is not difficult. Everyone does it unconsciously as he reads his newspaper or views pictures of current events. It is much more difficult, however, to imagine all the different factors which affect any given situation or problem. Anyone who makes the most superficial study of international relations is appalled by their complexity. He can sympathize with the foreign minister who fumbles or hesitates in forming a policy when faced with such considerations as defense, economics, public sentiment, and alternative but mutually exclusive proposals. Positive action of any sort is sure to offend some person or group.

The complexity of international problems, however, has a fortunate side. Competing proposals tend to "cross-pollinate" each other and to generate new ideas. That all nations are caught between competing alternatives implies that any nation is capable of persuasion if alternatives are sufficiently explored and matched together. In short, international relations is not dealing with monolithic entities. *Nations are people!*

The world scope of Rotary provides an opportunity for each Rotarian to make a significant contribution in this "exploring and matching" process. Within Rotary there is frankness which may be lacking in communications on the official level. In this respect the Rotarian who explores a problem with a Rotarian in another country may gain a more flexible impression of what that country really wants. At the same time he may be spared the disillusionment that occurs when verbal declarations are not followed by appropriate action. Instead of feeling ill-will, he will understand.

Another advantage derived from the complexity of international affairs is the ever-present possibility of technical solutions. We live in a technical age. Science can be blamed as the source of many of our troubles, but science never submits to a stalemate in its quest for answers. No group has been more resolute, for instance, in its attack upon the problem of international control of atomic energy than the scientists who produced the bomb.

Consider, for example, the case of water rights in the Punjab. The boundary line of partition cuts across the Indus river system, leaving most of the canals in Pakistan and the headwaters and the controlling canal works in India. Dispute over use of the waters has been one of the most serious problems dividing the two nations. Then, engineers came up with a scheme for using the wasted waters which might satisfy both countries. Said one of the engineers: "It's the method of thinking that counts. To get people to look at a canal as a canal, a problem in engineering— and not as a political controversy—that is the important step."

To seek and develop common grounds for agreement with peoples of other lands implies a willingness to project oneself into the often seemingly incomprehensible thought patterns of other nations and the resolution to explore all sorts of complicated technical solutions. The key word in this context is *develop*. Development implies *effort* and *time*. A number of international disputes have been under discussion for years without much progress, and public opinion, especially in the countries directly concerned, tends to become impatient. It has been led to expect perfect—and quick—solutions. Why?

Part of the answer to this question can be found in the system of mass communications upon which the public depends for most information and part of it can be answered by the method of negotiation itself.

23

Generally speaking, *conference* is the accepted pattern of negotiation—bringing the interested persons together around a table. Then, the scene begins to develop; behind each national delegate is a little knot of experts representing officials not present but actively interested in the negotiations; further back are rows of interested spectators drawn from all walks of life, by motives ranging from the earnest to the frivolous. Representatives of the press are present; television lights are glaring, and radio networks carry each syllable to the ends of the earth. Presto! The statesmen's dream—"open diplomacy."

This dream grew out of resentment against the cynical character of private negotiations. It was believed that honesty could be preserved by submitting transactions of nations to public view. Besides, the people had a right to know.

However, there were temptations in this picture which had not been foreseen. The diplomat turned delegate was often revealed as an eager propagandist, full of angry tirades and more or less subtle prevarications. If he showed the slightest tendency to reach an understanding with an opponent, he risked being called an "appeaser" by some indignant editorialist or opposition politician. Under these circumstances only a statesman with the stature of a Churchill would dare to urge a return to the practice of secret diplomacy. Sir Winston declared on one occasion:

> This conference should not be overhung by ponderous or rigid agenda or led into mazes or jungles of technical details zealously contested by hordes of experts and officials drawn up in a vast cumbrous array.

The conference should be confined to the smallest number of persons and powers possible. They should meet with a measure of informality and a still greater measure of privacy and seclusion.

It may well be that no hard and fast agreement would be reached but there might be a general feeling among those gathered together that they might do something better than tear the human race, including themselves, into bits.

Does this counsel present some hope of removing the impasse which now obstructs the path of conciliation? Proponents argue that the public would be freed from the confusion and uncertainty created by open diplomacy and consequent chronicling of a new crisis in every headline.

On the other hand, the public has a duty to be informed—a right to be present when its fate is being debated. Proponents of open diplomacy opine with equal vigor that pressure from constituents helps to raise the level of statesmanship, that in the long pull it is the one best hope for people-to-people diplomacy.

The daring person—and it must be clear that he is the daring one—who would follow the path of conciliation must also possess patience. Patience tempers conviction with the long breath and saving grace of common sense. It sustains the imagination in seeking to understand the other fellow's point of view and in the examination of difficult technical problems. Above all, patience is needed to deal with objections of the public at delicate stages of negotiations against being betrayed—"sold down the river" —accepting anything less than perfect solutions.

The very nature of the quest for common grounds excludes the possibilities of perfect solutions. No unconditional surrender, no victory for one side or the other can be expected. Little is gained by taking votes if the effect is to isolate a minority and harden its resistance. The task of conciliation is to devise alternative solutions based on whatever areas of agreement may be discovered through sympathetic efforts to understand.

Many persons are inclined to regard this task as one for mechanics—a precision job like putting an automobile together. Better suited, perhaps, are the gifts of a gardener who knows that he can only cultivate the ground, or change the atmosphere, and thus encourage growth. He must conform to nature, pruning a little here and fertilizing a little there. Mechanics armed with blueprints could accomplish little in transforming a wilderness. But a patient gardener, conscious of his limitations, can produce results.

"One of the most impressive examples of the possibilities of international co-operation," wrote a Rotarian, "is to be seen in one of those gardens wherein we find plants, shrubs and trees from all over the globe flourishing and flowering side by side in perfect harmony and beauty, to create between them that atmosphere wherein it is generally agreed that man comes nearest to his Maker.

"There is much wisdom to be learned in a garden, and the very beginning of that wisdom is a realization that all final results depend upon proper preparation of the soil. So it is with Rotary. The crop we envisage is world peace and stability. The seed to be sown—fellowship and friendship, understanding, good will, and good faith. The soil—the minds and thinking processes of individual Rotarians; and first in importance comes the preparation of the soil. . . ."

3

The Path of Freedom

*He will defend the rule of law and order to
preserve the liberty of the individual so that
he may enjoy freedom of thought, speech and
assembly, freedom from persecution and aggression, and freedom from want and fear.*[*]

FREEDOM IS A basic element of civilized society; it is one
of the principles enunciated by most governments today.
More words have been written and spoken about freedom than about most subjects—and, yet, few topics have
suffered more in the hands of men who, consciously or unconsciously, have used, and are using, it as an ideological
tool to advance selfish causes.

The political, economic, and religious implications of
freedom must be left to larger volumes and to more philo-
sophical discussions, but Rotarians are deeply concerned

[*] From the Outline of Policy in International Service.

about freedom. They have expressed themselves in word and deed about it.

The importance attached to freedom by Rotarians is amply demonstrated by the amount of attention given to it in the Outline of Policy in international service. Preceding the most pointed statement, quoted at the opening of this chapter, is a full delineation of what Rotarians mean by "freedom":

> The Rotary ideal of service finds expression only where there is liberty of the individual, freedom of thought, speech and assembly, freedom of worship, freedom from persecution and aggression, and freedom from want and fear.
>
> Freedom, justice, truth, sanctity of the pledged word and respect for human rights are inherent in Rotary principles and are also vital to the maintenance of international peace and order and to human progress.

Why this deliberate emphasis? It can be explained only by the importance that the compilers of the Outline, fortified by their consultation with Rotarians in many parts of the world, attached to the principle that is invoked. Liberty of the individual, his dignity and freedom of thought, have special meanings for Rotarians. When freedom is destroyed, order and progress go with it.

With the growth of totalitarian government in Europe and Asia between the world wars, Rotary clubs became targets of persecution. In one country a policy of total regimentation led to the disbanding of Rotary clubs. In another, Rotarians were jailed for "dangerous thoughts" because their membership in an "International" was suspect. In another place Rotary was suppressed by "a new political philosophy which has overcome individual thought as the structural defect of a whole epoch, and has replaced it by community-conscious thought."

The challenge to the integrity of Rotary was confronted squarely and openly in annual convention—the only place and time where the organization takes concerted action. At the Havana (Cuba) convention in 1940, a resolution declared that *where freedom, justice, truth, sanctity of the pledged word, and respect for human rights do not exist, Rotary cannot live nor its ideals prevail.*

Although Rotary has no secrets, no ritual, no rigid uniformity, it was in fact a symbol of freedom to dictators. Retreat rather than advance became the order of the day in countries where governments assumed totalitarian powers and recognized in Rotary an agency that could not be controlled for the purposes of propaganda and persecution. Before the outbreak of the second world war, Rotary was the target of official directives in several countries.

In spite of obstacles produced by daylight raids, blackouts, and flying bombs, many Rotary clubs continued to meet. The stimulus to thoughtfulness and helpfulness increased as Rotarians picked their way among the ruins. During the blitz itself the Rotary Club of London formed several new clubs within the territory originally assigned to it. Around the world, great international projects were initiated for the relief of victims of war, and for aid to prisoners and extending hospitality to troops far from home. Most dramatic picture, perhaps, of Rotary in a world at war was the report of an eye witness of a Rotary meeting that took place during an island invasion:

"In the semi-darkness of a stinking tunnel, met a group of seven Rotarians, with wounded men writhing in agony around them. The only civilian with them was the club president who had escaped . . . in a small boat. He rapped the table with his gavel, the butt of a pistol he had snatched from the soldier next to him, and called the meeting of what was left of the Rotary club to order."

So, in the face of struggle and suppression, the concern remained for something which meant *freedom*. Some Rotary clubs continued to meet secretly under other names. One club, for instance, became a choir and named itself for the grouse—which does not sing. Another club met regularly in a restaurant frequented by enemy officers. The records of many Rotary clubs were seized, and the president of at least one club was imprisoned for being a Rotarian.

After the war there was a rapid revival of Rotary in countries where it had been suppressed. The eagerness with which clubs sought the restoration of their charters after the war can be attributed partly to the stand taken by Rotarians in convention at Havana in 1940. It was clear that, once conditions were right, nothing need delay the resumption of fellowship and voluntary service. The much-lamented absence of Rotary clubs in certain countries does not represent any decision by Rotary International; it is the conditions in these countries which exclude Rotary.

Obviously, the Rotarian has a special reason for being drawn toward the path of freedom; namely, the preservation of Rotary, besides much else that he holds dear—perhaps *all* else. Never in human history was the issue more clearly drawn. Between a dark age of despotism and a golden age of freedom every man must choose, and often he may find that the foes of freedom are "they of his own household." The battle is not only along national lines. There is a fifth column within the gates—perhaps within his own mind. There is the temptation to defend freedom by denying freedom to those who seem to betray it.

A visitor to the unpretentious flat in Rome where lived Prime Minister de Gasperi was shocked by the blare of a phonograph in the next apartment. It was playing "Giovinezza," the Fascist anthem, the marching song of the party which had imprisoned de Gasperi and reduced his family to starvation. The prime minister shook his head ruefully. "It's the Countess," he explained. "She's trying to relieve my boredom and solitude by playing her records. Until now, she only played them at seven o'clock when she knew I was getting up to go to the office, and again at nine in the evening when I came home for dinner. But since my illness she plays them all day long; 'Giovinezza' . . . 'To Arms' . . . 'Hymn to Rome' . . . 'The Empire.'"

"You should complain!"

"I have," replied de Gasperi. "I even wrote a letter to Premier de Gasperi, signed by myself and all my family. But Premier de Gasperi answered that as head of a free government he is bound to respect individual liberties, including the right to play one's favorite songs and that therefore he could not possibly interfere in any private citizen's affairs."

How far should, or can, a free society go in giving personal freedom pre-eminence? Teachers often illustrate for children by saying that "your personal freedom ends where your playmate's freedom begins." Where is that? At what point must individual freedom be subjugated to the will of the group?

What, indeed, does *freedom* mean in the diverse regions of the world?

At the end of the second world war an American correspondent attended a luncheon in Europe where several Russians were also in attendance. He found himself seated between a Russian military photographer and a Russian interpreter. The photographer was recounting achievements of the Russian army, and the American turned to the interpreter: "Ask him what he thinks this war was all about."

The interpreter asked the question of the photographer, and the answer came forth like a bullet. "*Svoboda!*" said the Russian—"Freedom!" As if to say to the American, "Didn't you know—you poor ignorant fellow."

"Ask him—what *is* freedom?" the American said.

"Freedom"? answered the Russian, hesitating, then firmly—"Freedom is knowing how to help the other fellow. . . ."

Around the world in scores of places men are struggling for freedom, and the goals of freedom have been confiscated by men whose actions contradict their concern. Admitting that part of the problem is one of semantics, the fact is that freedom means a hundred different things to a hundred different people.

The problem of definition was demonstrated when representatives of 58 nations joined to explore the meaning of freedom. They combed through history and traditions, through famous documents in the struggle for liberty around the world. They disputed over phrasings and implications, and although after more than two years their Declaration of Human Rights was approved by 48 nations and opposed by none (10 nations abstained), the dispute is by no means over.

For the Rotarian who would "defend the rule of law and order to preserve the liberty of the individual" the Universal Declaration of Human Rights presents an interesting opportunity. Rotary International was among the first organizations to provide copies to its member clubs for discussion. Rotary clubs in many countries organized debates in their communities. Studies by international service committees were published in pamphlet form. Scores of radio stations broadcast panel discussions by Rotarians on the theme of human rights. Schools were invited to organize essay contests with prizes awarded by Rotary clubs, and the anniversary of the Declaration's adoption (10 December) has been observed in various ways.

While defenders of freedom have made abundant use of the Declaration as an educational device for clarifying and confirming the concept of freedom, subsequent attempts to establish the rule of law through an international covenant of human rights and measures of implementation have aroused the disquiet of some. A primary objection is that different nations have advanced further than others in giving effect to different aspects of freedom through domestic legislation and popular consent, and, under these circumstances, to agree on a legal formulation acceptable to all nations tends to produce the lowest common denominator. If it is to be acceptable to all, it is likely to be satisfactory to none. Such a watered-down formulation of freedom, it is alleged, might actually weaken the existing protections of human rights in some countries.

Rotary clubs which have proved their vigilance in pointing to this danger also suggest that public opinion in the community is the critical factor in preserving freedom. International agreement on definitions of freedom and procedures of implementation have little or no meaning unless there is capacity and willingness to understand the meaning of freedom at the community level.

Rotary clubs provide a forum in which freedom and human rights can be thoroughly discussed. From such deliberations the individual Rotarian can form his own conclusions based upon the principles of Rotary, upon conditions in his own community, and upon his own—and his friends'—insight. He will, or will not, defend the principles of freedom *where he is*. No international policing could possibly protect the rights of almost three billion persons—3,000 million individuals. Primary responsibility, therefore, must be in the local community and it is there, in his own home town, that the influence of the Rotarian in defense of human rights can be most usefully exerted.

One line of the defense of freedom—freedom of discussion—is in the weekly meeting of the Rotary club. Here, in the friendly atmosphere of Rotary, is a proper place for exchange of views. True, the controversial nature of many problems—especially international problems—presents difficulties and dangers, but is it not one of the goals of Rotary membership to replace political passion with a desire for understanding? We cannot escape controversial issues. How we face them is one measure of the club's mettle.

"I love the subdued chuckle that runs through a club," said the president of a Rotary club in England. "I love the subdued murmur of dissent." This is the atmosphere of Rotary—friendly, familiar fellowship which bears up under strong difference of opinion.

A past president of Rotary International declared:

> Divergence of view is the very pith of Rotary. In church and trade association we explore ideas with people we agree with. The germ of Rotary is bringing different kinds of men together; the butcher, the baker, the lawyer, the

doctor. Through differences, not similarities, Rotary seeks understanding. Because in Rotary we disagree without being disagreeable, many differences are resolved. But the fundamental is not that we must agree, only that we must explore and inform our minds so that our service to society as we go out of our meeting may be informed, intelligent service.

Rotarians have not only used the weekly meeting to stimulate thinking and to demonstrate the use of freedom; they have also adopted—or adapted—other types of meetings for the same purpose. The "fireside meeting," or "porch meeting" in warmer climes, has become a basic part of the techniques of Rotary. A wide range of topics has claimed the attention of Rotarians and their families in these informal, home meetings. The same is true in inter-city meetings, in inter-city general forums, and in other similar meetings organized to meet local needs and tastes.

In all such assemblies Rotarians have learned the value of personal participation; they are in increasing numbers substituting their own members for the imported "expert speaker." Experts have their places, but Rotarians have learned that in this age of wide and rapid communications, with the availability of books and magazines and with easy access to other Rotarians in other lands, more Rotarians can—and must—become *experts* themselves.

An editor of a weekly bulletin in one club which made this discovery wrote:

We should have no attendance problems if all our programs were like the one we had last week. It was a surprise for many of us to discover how much talent and wisdom there is among our own members. And best of all, we need have no hesitation in getting back at them. Last week's discussion went on long after the meeting. It is still going on.

If Rotarians are convinced that what they think is important enough to be stated publicly, they are likely to attach more value to what others think and say, and urge them to say it—which may be as important a facet of freedom as any other.

Adolph A. Berle, Jr., for example, opines that all that constitutions, statutes, and courts can do is to preserve "rights" as permissions. The more dangerous threat, he says, is the piling up of forces in society which influence men not to make use of these permissions:

> They are the deadening forces which give every motive to an individual not to let his thought range, not to disagree, not to open unpleasant questions, not to shock or displease the group in which he moves. They add up to a sort of paralyzing miasma of opinion which seems to think men's lives and thoughts should come into the world without shock and leave it without velocity. . . .
>
> In the more sophisticated societies, the danger to freedom comes from lethargy and conformity—what Goethe called "the deadly commonplace that fetters us all"—while in many parts of newly developing regions the danger comes from too aggressive a concern for freedom—a passion for forcing freedom upon men who are not prepared to use it wisely and well.

Whatever may be the situation in a given nation, Rotarians in more than 100 countries and geographical regions are in a challenging position to demonstrate and to transmit principles of freedom on whatever level is called for—always within the framework of Rotary policy.

Since the end of the second world war more than 650 million people have been given independence—freedom. And there are millions more who are gathering to march toward freedom. There was a time when these millions received their freedom from others, but now the cause of freedom has become, in the words of Tom Paine, "the cause of all mankind."

To millions who do not have it, and want it desperately, freedom is a bright hope and a rallying cry; to the few who fear it, it is more terrible than death; to those who have it, and cherish it, freedom is the foundation of human dignity and one of the paths to peace and plenty.

But there are those who fear it—even though they give lip service to it. During the years that 650 million persons received some kind of freedom in the form of independence, the same number, or more, were slipping behind various curtains of totalitarianism. Further, millions of persons in newly developing lands who wanted, first of all, to be themselves, were confused as to where they should fit in the world scheme. The problem was fairly stated by an American, the late Russell Davenport, who wrote: "Our idea of freedom does not seem to fit either the needs or the ideals of most of the people of the globe. There is something lacking in it that people want, something that they need, something that must sound in our words if our doctrine of freedom is to ring true. And we had now better find out what that 'something' is. For unless we can produce it communism will wholly capture, and will absorb, the cause of all mankind.

"There are 'experts' in the theory of freedom," he continued, "as there are today experts in everything; but they are inclined to speak a highly specialized language of their own, a step removed from the ken of ordinary mortals. It is to the ordinary mortal, not the expert . . . to whom we refer. . . . We have in mind those millions of persons who do not pretend to any special learning outside of their own professions, but who are nevertheless forced by the exigencies of democratic life, not only to think for themselves, but to provide leadership for others. . . ."

He might have been speaking of Rotarians—Rotarians who assemble, discuss, write, worship, work, and *lead*. They are in the vanguard of those who understand freedom, those who know that freedom, in the words of Thornton Wilder, is "a severe summons." If freedom is to be held against surprise attack or against the insidious encroachments of conformity, the cost will be more than the proverbial "eternal vigilance." The price has gone up.

The price is *study, search, defend, serve*—and the realization that freedom is more than *having* something: it is *living* something and wanting others to have it, too. Freedom is action *for*—not *against*; it is positive, vibrant, meaningful. It is indivisible, for in this age whenever freedom is denied to anyone anywhere, the freedom of everyone everywhere is in danger.

No nation can claim that it fully guarantees freedom and the protection of individual dignity. True, some are trying harder than others, but no person, no nation, has a right to boast. Freedom is a developing concept—a goal far out in advance of society—at the end of a path strewn with rocky detours. But that path is worth following, for it leads upward.

One of India's great poets, Tagore, said it well and for all mankind when he wrote:

Where the mind is without fear and the head is held high;
Where knowledge is free;
Into that land of freedom, my Father, let my
Country awake.

4

The Path of Progress

He will support action directed towards im-
proving standards of living for all peoples,
realizing that poverty anywhere endangers
*prosperity everywhere.** *

DURING THE PERIOD when the first satellites were launched,
a Rotarian—as did millions of others—read in the newspapers that one of the satellites would pass over his community at a certain time that evening.

"I walked into my back yard a few minutes ahead of
time," he said, "hardly convinced that the satellite would be
on schedule or that I would be able to see it. As I sat there
in the quiet setting of my yard with its familiar trees, flow-
ers, and shrubs, it seemed a strange place to be viewing this
new phenomenon. . . . I looked up again, toward the
northeast, and there it was—a good-sized star, it seemed,

* From the Outline of Policy in International Service.

streaking across the sky. I watched it race across the heavens—at 18,000 miles an hour—and disappear into the horizon. . . .

"The next night," he went on, "I worked late at the office, but I had read in the newspaper that the satellite would cross our town again that night. I forgot all about it, however, until I was driving home. I looked at my watch and found that it was almost time, at that moment, for it to pass over. I happened to be near a small park, so I quickly stopped the car and ran into the park, so that I could see a greater expanse of the sky. . . . I scanned the northern skies, and there it was, as large and as bright as ever—plunging across the star-lit heavens. I looked at my watch. It was within 30 seconds of the time the astronomers had predicted it would pass over! I could have set my watch by it—as we used to set our watches by the 5:30 train! Within the next hour, my friends across the whole earth would be looking up to see it, too, marveling as I was at the portent of a new age. I walked very slowly back to my car, hardly aware of the awesome beauty of the night—the moon, the stars, the quiet rustle of leaves, and the unbroken serenade of crickets. Another kind of awe had almost overcome me. . . ."

This was, in truth, the symbol of a new age—the Space-Atomic Age, and millions of persons stand in awe of it. To what does it lead? An age of peace and plenty? An age of confusion, imbalance, and struggle? Or what?

No matter what may become this age's ultimate goals and techniques for achieving them, historians agree that this age has another name which reveals the magnitude of the challenge: the Age of Great Expectations. The streaking satellite plunging across the heavens—unaware of national, racial, religious, economic, social, or cultural differences or boundaries—has become a symbol of technology and material progress. It is not the proper symbol of mankind's noblest and greatest genius, for these impulses belong to the spirit; but the hungry, the dispossessed, the ignorant, the "peasant three-quarters of mankind" of whom Toynbee speaks—these persons have caught the vision of technology and material progress.

An item so fundamental as food is a primary concern. Then, there is water and a roof and a bed. Things a quarter of the world takes for granted are things which three-quarters of the world has never had. Ten years after the second world war, after all the grandiose plans and costly projects of reconstruction, the number of hungry people in the world had actually increased! Half the people in the world earn less than $100 (£35) a year.

The average life expectancy at birth among two-thirds of the earth's inhabitants is little more than 30 years. Nearly half the human race cannot read or write. In many areas, there has been no substantial improvement in living standards during the last thousand years, and in several places conditions of life have actually declined.

Can the earth feed a growing population which is edging toward 3,000 million? Authorities disagree. Certainly there are problems of distribution even if production problems could be solved. But British geographer L. Dudley Stamp contends that "if the best current farm practices were used only in that area of the earth now cultivated, a population of at least 3,000 million could be nourished adequately. If the lands at present unused or inadequately used could be brought into production on the same basis, world population could climb to over 10,000 million. At the same time,

41

science is adding constantly to the sum of human knowledge, and there is every reason to expect advances that will simplify the problem of feeding the human race if only man can overcome the barriers he himself has erected between the nations." This, of course, is one scientist's view—and one with which many others are in sharp dissent. Some believe that the world is losing the race between conservation and disaster.

Where does the Rotarian fit in this picture? Can he make a contribution here? Freedom, according to the Outline of Policy, is *also vital to the maintenance of international peace and order and to human progress,* and now the Rotarian is admonished to *support action directed towards improving standards of living for all peoples* as his particular contribution in the path of progress.

The belief in progress is not easily sustained in the aftermath of two world wars, with awareness of all the barriers which have been erected between nations and of conditions under which most of mankind is forced to live. Perhaps faith in progress is an illusion, anyway.

If it is, then it should be clear that it is one more widely shared than ever before. The belief in continuous and inevitable material improvement, which was limited in the past to the western nations, has now become the primary goal of peoples in the most backward areas of the earth. Through the ferment of war and political struggle, they have been seized with a conviction that the benefits of science and technology can also come to them. And it is clear to the most superficial observer that these benefits will come. *How* they come—who will bring them, and where, and in what manner—this is where the Rotarian fits.

In any such process it must be understood that progress

is not a result of mere wishful thinking; less developed peoples can have no illusions on that score. Improving their standards of living demands from them the most strenuous efforts and much sacrifice to accumulate capital, to educate their people, and often to change drastically the forms of social life. But no matter how great their efforts, they are not sufficient of themselves. Help must come from those peoples who have experienced progress, who have the "know-how," the accumulated resources to invest and, above all, the will to help. The Outline of Policy assumes that the Rotarian possesses that will to help.

Volumes could be filled with evidence to justify this assumption. The ideal of service professed by Rotarians is no empty pose. On countless occasions they act to help others, not only in their own communities and countries but also when the appeal comes from abroad.

"He giveth twice who giveth quickly" might have been the motto of the small Rotary club which rushed carpentry and masonry tools to earthquake-stricken Ecuador. To these Rotarians the Rotary district governor of the recipient district addressed his appreciation:

> Your most interesting letter has been translated into Spanish and will be sent to every club of my district that they may learn how these modern Greeks of Rotary can work wonders in spite of small numbers.

> At the same time, I fear that we have imposed on your generosity a task out of all proportion: hammers, trowels, saws, nails, often from the very orderly tool chest of Madame Rotarian. . . . How abusive and preposterous! And then the cumbersome chore of packing and shipping them for the benefit of the descendants of the Inca empire. . . . We realize fully the magnitude of your effort and its significance. The name of your club will always be held by the

43

Rotarians of our district as a beacon to show us the right path of international relations.

We are planning to construct something permanent such as a school for children or a hospital pavilion that will be maintained by the clubs of our district as a lasting memento to the munificence of Rotary International.

Vision and energy have poured forth time and again from Rotary clubs to elicit responses as warm as that cited above. They have spearheaded community drives for funds, food, and clothing. Year after year, supplements to meager rations overseas have been sent regularly, often as the product of austerity luncheons and other forms of self-denial. The forgotten people—victims of aggression in Korea, Vietnam refugees, escapees in Berlin and along the Hungarian border—have benefited from Rotary thoughtfulness. The need has only to be made known as a practical opportunity for helping and Rotarians have taken action.

Yes, Rotary can rise to an emergency, and for the long haul, too, Rotarians can sustain their efforts as was manifested by British Rotary clubs in a two-year campaign which netted £100,000 ($280,000) in aid to villages devastated in the Greek civil war. Tens of thousands of families were rehabilitated; 100,000 children were clothed and given medical attention; whole villages were restored.

The will to help is abundantly manifest, but is this action of a kind to improve standards of living for all peoples? To draw an analogy from local experience, consider the case of a family in your town that has been visited by catastrophe, perhaps the death of its bread-winner. Rallying support for this family is comparable to action which has been described in the international field. Quite different is the equally common instance of the local youth who wants to go into business for himself or needs some training to make him more productive. Rotarians have ways of helping in this case, too, and this is the kind of help needed in the newly developing countries. Are Rotary clubs and Rotarians in a position to support efforts to supply that kind of help?

Indeed they are, and in many different ways.

Echoes from the Outline of Policy can be detected in the Act for International Development (U.S. Public Law 535):

> The peoples of the United States and other nations have a common interest in the freedom and in the economic and social programs of all peoples. Such progress can further the secure growth of democratic ways of life, the expansion of mutually beneficial commerce and the development of international understanding and good will and the maintenance of world peace.

A past president of Rotary International was a member of the advisory board that initiated the Act, and 43 Rotarians worked as legislators for its passage. Among its fruits have been missions of technical assistance to 60 countries requesting aid in the development of their resources. The program is currently employing some 2,000 experts in production, processing, distribution, and administration. Five thousand apprentice technicians have come to the United States for training.

The United States is not alone in undertaking this type of program. There is also the Colombo Plan for cooperative development in Asia. France is active in the field, and even quite small countries have their own expert aid. Some 80 countries contribute to United Nations technical assistance through the specialized agencies concerned with agriculture, health, and education.

Rotarians have allies and examples in international service in the persons enlisted for these programs. Personal acquaintance is the genius of their work, for the expert who has not the gift of associating and communicating with the people of the country he is helping to develop finds himself greatly handicapped. Many of those working in technical assistance are Rotarians or become members of Rotary clubs, if they are qualified for membership, in the countries where they are working. Being in Rotary, they report, greatly increases their effectiveness.

One Rotarian poses an interesting challenge. Could not individual volunteers for this service be found among the hundreds of thousands of business and professional men who have passed the retirement age? They have the technical experience needed. Their minds are flexible and their health vigorous. They may resent being put on the shelf after they have trained others to take their place. They might well share their technical abilities with peoples struggling to raise their standards of living.

"Aside from helping the needy areas," he concludes, "these men would get a tremendous personal satisfaction from it; increase their active lives a dozen years or more; and returning home could tell the folks about the wonderful people abroad. . . ."

If circumstances prevent a Rotarian from accepting such a challenge, there are other ways in which he can lend his support. He can set out to inform himself and others about the need for improving living standards. Public ignorance, especially in the so-called "advanced" countries, is deplorable. Few realize the meagerness of the resources available in comparison with what needs to be done. Another past president of Rotary International, chairman of his country's legislative committee on atomic energy, calls on every Rotary club to devote four programs a year to discussing peaceful uses of the atom. Only a quickened public awareness, he feels, can surmount the rocks and shoals which infest the course of the atomic age.

Information is only the first step. The individual Rotarian or a Rotary club alerted to problems can make substantial contributions. The boy who benefited from a student loan and became co-inventor of a process which promises to make atomic power as plentiful as heavy hydrogen in the oceans is a source of pride to the Rotary club that sponsored him. Training in all fields of science can be encouraged to meet the urgent call for technical abilities.

A sense of participation in mankind's march of material progress can be fostered through supporting one of the public or private agencies seeking to improve living standards. In several countries, Rotary clubs have taken the lead in calling attention to the United Nations Children's Fund (UNICEF). They are able to show how far a little money will go, not only in feeding the hungry but also in checking disease. For one dollar, this agency can provide a dozen doses of penicillin to heal the horrible sores inflicted by yaws upon the bodies of children. For the same amount, a hundred children can be immunized from tuberculosis with the BCG vaccine. It is hoped that this scourge can soon be virtually eliminated, and similar results are sought in the campaign against malaria, another great destroyer of human life and vigor. Spraying swamps with insecticide can free for cultivation huge areas now lost in the battle for bread.

It may be that co-operation in the path of progress also can be undertaken through the world fellowship of Rotary. Many a Rotary club in Asia has adopted a neighboring village festering in squalor and want. Many more such redemptive efforts might be undertaken if assistance were forthcoming from Rotary in other countries. To share in them would honor any Rotary club, for these Rotarians are *giving of themselves* in this cause. Description of this typical scene comes from India:

> We cannot fail to have some satisfaction that after a couple of months of planning and spade work, we started our work on the Rotary village in right earnest. Most of the members present dug trenches for dumping the refuse of their adopted village. After this we started on a bathing day for the village children. All were given a lesson in cleaning their teeth. Their dirty clothes were taken off and Rotarians gave the children a thorough rub with soap and warm water. While this was going on, hot milk prepared from powder was given to every child after his bath. What an exhilerating feeling these children must have had after their bath and warm glass of milk!

Simple things . . . fundamental things . . . providing sanitation, housing, cottage industries and, above all, education. Numerous examples—and the number is growing—can be cited in which these village people have had their feet set upon the path of material progress. It is not necessarily a matter of *doing* the work which needs to be done—it is giving "know-how" to people so that they can help themselves. More local Rotary aid might be given if it were known that help would come from Rotarians in other places. A club anywhere might help train and send a technician to work in these newly developing countries.

To supply tools for fundamental education in the less

developed countries, many Rotary clubs have been presented with UNESCO Gift Coupons by Rotarians abroad.
These are used to purchase equipment for training people
to help themselves. A little girl in The Netherlands was
surprised to hear from an adviser of the Food and Agriculture Organization working in the foothills of the Hima-
layas. She had been one of several thousand children who
had contributed to the purchase of gift coupons for a laboratory in the State of Uttar Pradesh. The writer recalled
how he had interested Dutch Rotarians in organizing the
drive for funds and explained how essential the equipment was to the development of this beautiful country and
its people. Members of the local Rotary club had helped
to build the laboratory, he told her, and ended his letter
with these words:

> So you see, Hanny, with your kwartje (quarter of a florin)
> you have contributed to better understanding which our
> world so badly needs. I thought of all this when I saw that
> scrap of paper with your name and address on it. Don't
> forget, Hanny, that if ever you are in trouble, and I hope
> that will never happen, you will always meet with help
> somewhere if only you remember this: dare to understand,
> dare to give and to act, dare to receive.

Could not this advice given to a child be extended to
all the peoples of the world? In the most vital sense, we
are members one of another.

There is no use in pretending, however, that small gestures of this kind can solve the problem alone. Multiplied
and spread over the many countries where there are Rotary clubs, they can provide a stimulus and a reassurance
to faith. Large government schemes can fail of their own
weight unless they have the eager support of public opin-

ion. Projects such as have been described make technical assistance a personal undertaking for those who co-operate in them. And in the receiving country, there is encouragement to work and sacrifice in the knowledge that people in a distant land are encouraging them in their struggle to improve their standard of living. These simple, tangible, practical acts of service contribute to the morale of progress, and morale is important.

The path of progress is beset with so many difficulties and weighted by so many controversial issues that it is all too easy to throw up one's hands in despair. Only the individual Rotarian can confront these questions squarely, study them in all their aspects, and support the action that reason and conscience dictate. In many ways, Rotarians are focusing attention upon these issues, making them the subject of debates and discussions at weekly meetings. Members gather in homes to explore them further. Through correspondence and exchange of programs with clubs in other countries, the knowledge and insights of world fellowship are brought to bear on them. Members address other organizations on these problems. Young minds in the schools are being taught to wrestle with them. In short, the Rotary club can exercise its function as an agency of public enlightenment.

What are some of these issues?

One of the most formidable is that of *investment*. Large resources must be devoted to improving standards of living; large resources must be devoted to enterprises in the newly developing countries. Some of these enterprises may quickly produce income, thereby being attractive to local capital or to business in other lands. On the other hand, there are many vital projects which yield no direct income or only small returns after many years. The costs of providing electric power, irrigation, and transportation, for example, often run far beyond the borrowing capacity of these governments. Yet such works must be undertaken if there is to be progress in the production of food, raw materials, and manufactured goods.

What should be the source of this capital? Should it be mobilized by governments through taxation? Or, is there some way in which private investors can be enlisted to support what must be, in the short run at least, a profitless undertaking? As businessmen, Rotarians are expected to provide enlightenment on this question and sound advice to the public when specific answers are proposed.

Another problem is *protection of investments.* What guarantees can be offered by newly-developing countries that capital from abroad will not be subject to excessive taxation—or even outright confiscation? This is a most sensitive point for nations which have recently established their independence. They insist on their right to sovereignty over their natural resources. But how can they expect to attract the large-scale investment from abroad required for their development if they do not definitely guarantee its protection?

Another issue is the *economic system* of the country itself. Can its stability be assured? Does it operate to the advantage of the majority of its citizens or for only a few? These are only a few questions bearing down upon humanity as it draws nearer together, through technology.

This "togetherness" is real. It exists—now. One quarter of humanity has been relieved of the struggle for food and water, and has thereby been released for the creation of the Good Life—at least on a material basis. This is the world of rapid communications, automation, jet transportation, and leisure. This is the world which has brought mankind to the Space Age.

To its credit, this world has also produced love and charity, freedom and compassion, vision and concern. The "inner space" has not been completely filled, but the process is going on. Rotarians are called to a concern for other peoples' "standard of living," but they are not unaware that the worst poverty of all is poverty of the human spirit.

Therefore, as three-quarters of the earth's population awakens to its new opportunities—as it crosses in a few decades what one-quarter has covered in centuries, it will have help and guidance. It must have the right kind of guidance, however, or the subsequent explosion will be indescribably tragic.

The historian Toynbee has summarized it in this way:

> Ever since man's passage from the Lower to the Upper Paleolithic stage of technological progress, the human race had been Lords of Creation on Earth in the sense that, from that time onwards, it had no longer been possible either for inanimate nature or for any other non-human creature either to exterminate mankind or even to interrupt human progress. Thenceforth, nothing on Earth, with one exception, could stand in Man's way or bring Man to ruin; but that exception was a formidable one—namely Man himself.

5

The Path of Justice

*He will uphold the principles of justice for
mankind, recognizing that these are fundamental and must be world-wide.**

THE GREAT CONVERSATION of Socrates and his friends in
The Republic begins with a discussion which, in content,
is as current as today's newspaper. Thrasymachus says, "I
proclaim that justice is nothing else than the interest of
the stronger. . . ."

Socrates is further compelled to defend his thesis that
justice is "among those goods which he who would be
happy desires both for their own sake and for the sake of
their results."

Glaucon counters, then, that "the life of the unjust is,
after all, better far than the life of the just."

The origin of justice as developed by Glaucon in a later

* From the Outline of Policy in International Service.

argument with Socrates is relevant here, because it accurately reflects how a sizable number of twentieth century men define justice.

Glaucon says justice is a compromise, "between the best of all, which is to do injustice and not be punished, and the worst of all, which is to suffer injustice without the power of retaliation; and justice, being at the middle point between the two, is tolerated not as a good, but as the lesser evil, and honored by reason of the inability of men to do injustice. . . ."

A second reading of Glaucon's definition may be necessary; reflection certainly is called for. The "best of all"—to do injustice and not be punished!

Does this sound familiar? *How far can we go and still be within the law? You're not very bright if you don't take advantage of him. We had better "get while the getting is good." Now is the time to hit him, while he's weak.*

Whether the field is business, international relations, home relationships, or any segment of life in which men must deal with each other, the temptation is great to call justice the "lesser evil." To anyone who reads the daily newspapers it must be clear that many persons succumb to Glaucon's "best."

A passionate sense of justice, however, seems indeed to be fundamental in human nature. Moved by it, men have not hesitated to "pledge their lives, their fortunes, and their sacred honor" in wars where each side was convinced that theirs was the cause of justice. Voltaire said: "The sentiment of justice is so natural and so universally acquired by all mankind, that it seems to be independent of all law, all party, all religion." Here is something universal, then, upon which men should be able to agree. But it is not easy. Kipling touched the heart of it with—

> The world is wondrous large, seven seas from marge to
>   marge,
> And holds a vast of various kinds of men;
> The wildest dreams of Kew are the facts of Khatmandu,
> And the crimes of Clapham, chaste in Martaban.

Under these circumstances, can *universal* principles be found? What are these principles of justice that the Outline of Policy calls upon the Rotarian to uphold? To be recognized as fundamental and as demanding application *world wide*, these principles must cover a vast territory, an infinite variety of values, and a great many opposing points of view which are passionately held. In a world where many disputes are settled by robbing Peter to pay Paul, and justice sometimes occupies the mourner's bench at peace conferences, these principles must have a superior logic to be capable of raising justice from the level of partisanship to the level of principle.

Can nations be so persuaded? Can the personal acquaintance that Rotary fosters between men of different nations help in the establishment of these universal principles of justice?

A visitor from the United States found his warmest welcome at a Rotary club in Scotland where one member took special pride in making visitors feel at ease. About 30 seconds after he had been introduced, this member called the visitor by his first name and said, "Lee, you are a remarkable American!"

"Thank you, sir," was the surprised response, "but I can't see how you can arrive at such a conclusion on such short acquaintance."

"Well," answered the host, "you speak Scottish so that

we can understand what you are trying to say, and that's remarkable. We Scots like you for that. Then I notice you don't drink Scotch at all, and that is remarkable, too. We like you very much on that account, for most visitors try to drink up all our Scotch."

From this humorous beginning, an intimate discussion developed at the luncheon table on the theme that "what the nations of the world need most is to try to look at every situation from the other man's direction."

From the other man's direction—this is the test. A proverb from the American Indian admonishes to this effect: "Do not condemn the other man until you have worn his moccasins." The challenge is to "get into the shoes" of the other person. Is there a way to do this, beyond the normal processes of reading, correspondence, discussions, hearing lectures, and travel?

There are other steps which can be taken—steps which involve action and putting knowledge to work. "Role-playing" is one device—pretending to be someone else or a representative of an organization or nation which embraces a point of view different from your own. Many Rotary clubs have used this as a program technique. Done well, it means thorough preparation by the participants and, just as important if there is to be open discussion, thorough preparation by members of the audience. To be specific, the technique might involve the club president or program chairman saying, "If you were an American, Abdullah, how would you feel about the recognition of communist China?" It may be quite a stretch of the imagination for Rotarian Abdullah to put himself into the shoes of an American—and vice versa—but the effort helps him escape from provincial limitations in his thinking.

Above all, it reveals that justice has at least two sides.

Carrying this technique one step further, several communities have organized into-their-shoes conferences, with local persons organized into groups of five to eight, each group to "represent" a nation in an international conference. They debated major world problems in a series of public meetings which went on over a period of several weeks.

Can a person engaged in such intensive study—writing to Rotarians in other lands to get firsthand information and defending "his country's" policy in public debate—really put himself "into the shoes" of another person thousands of miles away? The evidence says that he can and that it builds a new concept of justice and fair play.

One American representing Bolivia in this project went into his grocery store one morning and learned that the price of coffee had gone down. "My first reaction," he reported, "was—how terrible! South Americans can't afford to reduce their coffee price!"

There is another technique, previously cited, which has been developed by Rotarians—but widely used by non-Rotarians, too—which also works well as a "yardstick" for justice. It is "The Four-Way Test of the things we think, say, or do":

Is it the TRUTH?
Is it FAIR to all concerned?
Will it build GOOD WILL and BETTER FRIEND-
    SHIPS?
Will it be BENEFICIAL to all concerned?

Although this test was devised originally for use in a business faced with crisis and has been developed in Rotary initially as an adjunct to vocational service, it actually has wider application. Experience, indeed, has shown time and again that when a man earnestly uses The Four-Way Test in his business or profession, the results are also evident in his conduct as father, friend, and citizen. That this simple yardstick of human relations can be useful in international service also is the conviction of one Rotarian in The Philippines:

> In the promotion of Rotary's fourth avenue of service, the exemplification of The Four-Way Test in the diplomatic relations between nations will certainly exert a tremendous influence. The world is flooded with so much propaganda that confuses our minds and distorts our views. There is so much distortion of the truth that leads to misunderstanding and mutual animosities. I believe that a challenge is hurled at Rotary to diffuse the genius of The Four-Way Test through its fourth avenue of service.

Might not these four simple questions likewise prove helpful in the quest for universal principles of justice? Evidence of the usefulness of The Four-Way Test for this purpose is the fact that it has been accepted and adopted in most countries where there are Rotary clubs. It is not a code of ethics. No one can object to it because it merely reminds him to use his own best judgment. It does not tell him what to do. It merely asks him to look at what he thinks, says, or does in the light of his own standards. A principle of justice which is upheld by The Four-Way Test should, accordingly, be acceptable to all peoples.

The Rotarian who is exploring the path of justice may wish to undertake the testing for himself. A critical examination of his own principles of justice is one way of upholding them, of proving that they are more than high-sounding slogans. It may also reveal opportunities for him to help in making them world-wide.

To illustrate: what of the much discussed principle of self-determination? How does it meet The Four-Way Test? The *truth* is that this principle has carved for itself a formidable place in the history of our times. The most massive fact in world politics of this generation has not been the wars which claimed the headlines, but the achievement of self-rule by nearly half the human race. *Fair to all concerned*, surely, is the freedom of all peoples to pursue their own destinies, to make their own mistakes and their distinctive contributions to mankind. Once their independence is secured, moreover, the *good will* and *friendship* of these peoples seem to turn with special warmth toward their former officials. The *beneficial* results remain to be seen, but these new nations have high hopes and are spurred to great accomplishment.

The principle of self-determination would seem to meet The Four-Way Test. But to uphold a principle calls for more than passive approval. "Justice," said Disraeli, "is truth in action." Justice must surmount the real problems which are involved in making it world-wide. And there are many problems. One consequence of self-determination is the multiplication of nations, a "balkanization" such as occurred in Europe after the first world war—and held in part responsible for the second.

Today, there emerges a contrast between the growth of economic interdependence and the trend toward political independence. Further difficulties relate to the readiness for self-government. To many minds, a level of education enabling a new nation to function in the modern world is essential. Yet to others, this requirement is dubious.

For the individual Rotarian, opportunities leading to the path of justice arise in efforts to surmount these problems. Around the world, however, efforts are being made. They are as varied as the problems and the particular situations. In the new nations of Asia, Rotarians wrestle with the problems of achieving responsible external relations along the new frontiers. Individual Rotarians in Europe, perceiving the urgency of economic interdependence, have sought to supplant the tradition of separation of states by actively supporting the movement to unite Europe and to make "Europeans" out of the peoples of ancient states. This trend has found expression in the creation of the Coal and Steel Community, Euratom, and the Common Market.

The non-European committees of Rotary clubs in South Africa are active in helping the African to develop his competence for self-government without sacrificing his cultural integrity. In the Antipodes individuals who have manifested the principle of self-determination by emigration receive a Rotary welcome. It was a Rotary club that invented the description of them as "New Australians," which honors their status and pledges Rotarians to help them in realizing its promise.

Other principles of justice can be explored in similar fashion to discover opportunities for service in upholding them and making them world-wide. Throughout all of them is woven one topic: the development of international law. For the antithesis of justice in all human societies is the rule that might makes right. As Pascal put it, "Justice and power must be brought together, so that whatever is just may be powerful, and whatever is powerful may be just." The course of civilization has been the search for a rule of law to replace the creed of the caveman.

Mankind knows what he must do. The validity of Benjamin Franklin's argument is now clearer than ever:

Justice is as strictly due between neighbor nations as between neighbor citizens. A highwayman is as much a robber when he plunders in a gang as when single; and a nation that makes an unjust war is only a great gang of robbers.

Laws can be made to apply to the Space-Atomic Age. But the world community keeps returning to other—and outdated—concepts, anything to circumvent the rule of law. According to one historian, "the only way to make the mass of mankind see the beauty of justice is by showing them, in pretty plain terms, the consequence of injustice. . . ."

The latter consequences are becoming clearer with each passing day. A former president of the American Bar Association has said:

The atomic and hydrogen bombs have attuned the people of the world to an overwhelming desire for peace, stronger than any such desire in all history. Here a great opportunity will be won or lost. We lawyers must write the necessary legal machinery to maintain essential national sovereignty, yet provide for the peaceful settlement of disputes between nations under the rule of law. . . .

Even before the atomic and hydrogen bombs had pointed up the urgency of the task, the late U.S. Senator Taft saw with almost prophetic insight what must lie ahead:

I believe that in the long run the only way to establish peace is to write a law, agreed to by each of the nations, to govern the relations of such nations with each other and to obtain the covenant of all such nations that they will abide by that law and by decisions made thereunder.

The world community wavers uncertainly, however, before the entrance to the path of justice, somewhat like Sir Edward Coke when he confronted King James and blurted out, "The king is under God and the law"—and then fell to his knees in terror of losing his head.

"If men were angels," explained *The Federalist*, "no government would be necessary. In framing a government which is to be administered by men over men, the great difficulty lies in this: you must first enable the government to control the governed, and in the next place oblige it to control itself. . . ."

Oblige it to control itself. . . . If there is a problem which should engage the attention of every man, woman, and child in this generation, it is the need for development and application of international law. At stake is not merely the prevention of wars in an age when nations have acquired the means of total destruction, but also human advancement in all fields which the establishment of a sound system of international law would allow. Yet, for most people, international law is a remote subject, with no reference to their own survival and to the prospects for abundant life for themselves and their children.

Once more, the Outline of Policy challenges the individual Rotarian to practical endeavor. To uphold the principles of justice, to make them world-wide, he must inform himself and others not only about the present status of international law and the prospects for its development, but also about the sacrifices which the establishment of a rule of law might require. In bringing nations from the law of force to accept the force of law, a price must be paid, and little can be gained if it is ignored. The path of justice leads inevitably to the path of sacrifice.

Does not this situation suggest a specific task which is within the competence of any Rotary club? An intensive study under the guidance of members in the legal classification? Fireside meetings, club programs, public forums, into-their-shoes conferences—are these practical? How can public interest be created? Or, is it worth the struggle?

Historian Toynbee, after examining the history, development, and fall of various civilizations which have flowered, concludes:

> As a rule the demand for codification (of law) reaches its climax in the penultimate age before a social catastrophe, long after the peak of achievement in jurisprudence has been passed, and when the legislators of the day are irretrievably on the run in a losing battle with ungovernable forces of destruction. . . .

The path of justice leads around the world—into the backward villages, through the halls of government, and up to the "summit." It is, as Daniel Webster called it, "the ligament which holds civilized beings and civilized nations together."

Justinian, the great lawgiver, called justice "the constant desire and effort to render to every man his due."

It is unnecessary to point out that nations are like people, but the thought is an appropriate introduction to this story told by a journalist who had returned from a newly-developing land. With minor substitution of terms, this story might have happened anywhere:

> A poor shoemaker made a pair of shoes a day, which he sold for 63 cents. If he sold them in his own village, some person of a higher class might take them from him without paying at all. If he protested, he would be beaten. So he

preferred to walk a long distance to another market. It was a long walk in the hot sun, but it was worth it.

Then, he clinched his point that it was not a matter of money—in fact, the money was less important than something else: *justice*.

"I want justice," he declared. "I want to be treated as an equal. I want my dignity."

6

The Path of Sacrifice

*He will strive always to promote peace be-
tween nations and will be prepared to make
personal sacrifices for that ideal.*[*]

In 1958 *The Saturday Review* published a one-page article in the form of a contest announcement. In big and
bold type the headline proclaimed:

WORLD-WIDE COMPETITION
$1,000,000,000,000
IN TAX-FREE PRIZES

Then the details followed:

YOU ARE ALREADY ENTERED—

If your name begins with A, B, C, etc., or with Δ, ϕ, θ,
etc., or if you live in the U.S.A., Russia, France, etc., you

---

[*] From the Outline of Policy in International Service.

*are already entered in this competition. Your children, and
their children-to-be, are entered.*

THE PRIZES—

*The prizes, conservatively valued at $1,000,000,000,000,
include the following:*

A five-mile thick layer of pure, non-radioactive air.

Cities consisting of buildings, not rubble.

Water reservoirs not contaminated with fall-out.

Farmlands capable of growing edible food.

*Your home, car, TV set (and incidentally your life)—
and various extras, such as unlimited energy from the
atom and perhaps interplanetary travel.*

Then, a bit later this bombshell:

*How to Withdraw from the Competition: You Can't
EVER.*

And, finally—

*If You Want to Win: Help Find a Firm Road to Last-
ing Peace.*

In the previous chapter it was pointed out that the path
of justice leads inevitably to the path of sacrifice. It must
be apparent, first, that even to *speak* of peace entails an
element of sacrifice. At some time, and, for a few people,
the word *peace* has become tarnished with guilt by association—a mask for subversion, tyranny, and aggression.
Beware, they say, of those who cry "peace, peace" when
there is no peace.

Perhaps this bitter feeling only reflects in an extreme
form the general disappointment with the sequel to the
second world war. So much had been taken for granted.
There had been an unconditional surrender. Now there
was peace, and folks could go about their business and

enjoy themselves and leave the diplomats to worry about "foreign affairs."

Speaking to a Rotary club in England, an American ambassador put it this way:

> I went to the last war as many of you did, and I really believed we were fighting a war to end wars, and that we were fighting for democracy, and that our children would reap some of the benefit of the sacrifice made by our generation. . . . We did not really care enough in the intervening years. If we cared enough, we did not do enough or get enough done. It is rarely in the world's history that men get a second chance; and we have got a second chance.

What thoughtful observer of international service could not echo these sentiments and apply them to himself? They ring so true in this hour of history.

The last war came close to destroying civilization. Hunger and humiliation, social and economic disruption, the vacuum left by the defeated powers—all combined to produce a time of trouble and tension. Those who thought of peace as the end of a fairy tale where "they all lived happily ever after" were cruelly deceived. The cartoons which represented peace as an angel or a bride prepared the public mind for bitter disillusionment. On the contrary, peace should have been portrayed as the bride in real life—as a working girl with a tremendous job on her hands, compelled to "work at her marriage," as the counselors say, if it were to be a success.

This concept of peace as a summons to work rather than a license for personal irresponsibility is made quite explicit in the Outline of Policy with its call for *personal sacrifices*. But perhaps it was never driven home more poignantly than in the last public address of that valiant worker for international friendship, the late John Winant. Breaking into his prepared speech, he asked his audience abruptly:

"Are you giving as much today for peace as you gave for this country in the days of war?"

There was a pause before and after he spoke his own quiet answer:

"I am not."

Anyone looking back over the years since the war might so examine himself. In time of war, the urge to sacrifice is omnipresent, and personal efforts are measured by those who "give the last full measure of devotion." For purposes of destruction, the finest and most generous in human nature is expended. To save his country from destruction, however, and to secure peace, freedom, and the survival of all he holds dear, man is under no such compulsion.

Does this make sense?

Perhaps the extraordinary sacrifices of wartime are explained by the fact that many people respond best in a crisis. The exceptional and abnormal call forth the heroic in man. But is war the exception in human experience? History suggests the opposite conclusion. Over the sum of years, the abnormal experience has been the brief intervals of peace. Even the nineteenth century, which gave birth to the illusion of peace as a normal condition, was filled with little wars. In the twentieth, periods when the whole world was at peace can be measured only in months, not in years.

People in earlier ages might reflect that war, after all, was the business of a few knights or professional soldiers on isolated battlefields. During the Wars of the Roses, for example, at the moment when a battle was about to begin, the hue and cry of a hunt arose, and the armies withheld their attack while the fox, the hounds, and huntsmen streamed between them. Then they took up their own grim pastime.

If war was ever in fact so gentlemanly in its conduct, its nature has been utterly changed in modern times. War has become *total*, mobilizing entire peoples and their resources, aiming at total destruction. None can count himself immune. There is no place to hide. There are no more civilians. Children will become "combatants," the same as their elders.

Do not these circumstances demand a revised concept of war and peace? The late Albert Einstein, the mathematical genius who fathered the atomic age, projected the issue on the broadest scale and in the bluntest terms:

> A new type of thinking is essential if mankind is to survive and move to higher levels.
>
> Often in evolutionary processes a species must adapt to new conditions in order to survive. Today the atomic bomb has altered profoundly the nature of the world as we know it.
>
> The tank is a defense against bullets but there is no defense in science against the weapon which can destroy civilization.
>
> Our defense is not in armaments nor in going underground.
>
> Our defense is in law and order. In the light of new knowledge, the human race must adapt its thinking.

There is no easy optimism in the mood of the Rotarian who strives to promote peace, to halt and reverse the normal drift into war. He is disillusioned with cheap panaceas. He is a realist. He knows that victory in this struggle will not be won by subscribing to some pressure group or by passing a resolution in his club. The Rotarian must ask himself what personal sacrifices are required of him and his fellow men if mankind is to survive and move to higher levels.

Can anyone answer for him? Obviously, no, though he can be fortified and inspired through consultation with other earnest men. Ultimately, the answer must come from his own private conscience and be made manifest in his individual action. Here, only a few forms of sacrifice will be suggested as background for deliberation and discussion.

First, and perhaps most obvious of all, is the kind that falls at present on every taxpayer and burdens the economy of the entire world to the tune of $120,000,000,000 (£43,000,000,000) a year. In the wealthiest country of the world, "peace through strength" exacts a personal sacrifice from the average taxpayer equivalent to a month's salary. "Who desires peace, prepares for war" was the justification of this policy in ancient Rome. A most vigorous exposition of it in the twentieth century was given by a famous admiral:

> I am not for war, I am for peace. If you rub it in both at home and abroad that you are ready for instant action with every unit of your strength in the front line and intend to be first in and hit your enemy in the belly, and kick him when he is down, and boil your prisoners in oil if you take any, and torture his women and children, then people will keep clear of you.

Will they? This ancient form of sacrifice which is still so fashionable has not prevented wars. It has enhanced general insecurity, fomented an arms race and, finally, brought the use of the great deterrents—yesterday the admiral's dreadnaughts, tomorrow the guided missiles with hydrogen war-heads. Never was this policy more scathingly denounced than by the president of one country which had adopted it:

Every gun that is made, every warship launched, every rocket fired signifies in the final sense a theft from those who hunger and are not fed, those who are cold and are not clothed.

This world in arms is not spending money alone.

It is spending the sweat of its laborers, the genius of its scientists, the hopes of its children.

The cost of one modern heavy bomber is this: a modern brick school in more than thirty cities.

It is two fine and fully equipped hospitals.

And so on to the conclusion:

This, I repeat, is the best way of life to be found on the road the world has been taking.

This is not a way of life at all in a true sense. Under the cloud of threatening war, it is humanity hanging on a cross of iron.

If in one fell swoop the plague of war could be eradicated, what could a comparable amount of money, energy, and genius accomplish for mankind? The thought taxes the imagination! Is it possible in the wildest dream to conceive what $120,000 million (£43,000 million) a year could do, harnessed to policies of peace and service? Now, it is as if humanity were struggling up the stairs of civilization on one leg.

The path of sacrifice may indeed lead head-on into strongly entrenched traditions; there are those—and in large numbers—who say that history repeats itself, that today's humanity is no better than its forebears. "Wars and rumors of wars" there will always be. One answer is that our forebears were not attracted to the path of sacrifice, either; nor were they in the posture of Atomic-Age man. The real answer, however, has been given by another military man who states unequivocally that what mankind now requires is "an attack on the institution of war itself." A Rotarian from South America has put it this way:

> In accord with the object of Rotary, we should look into the deeper causes of war and of the diabolical motives that move men to kill each other; what statism impels them to do, what they abhor, and which they recognize as abominable and in contradiction of our ideal of service above self. . . . What is proposed is in no sense impossible nor calling for a superior intelligence, but an absolute necessity. The time to act is now.

Another Rotarian has stated: "Ours is a man-sized task which must be approached with the kind of genius and effort which went into the first atomic bomb. . . . Civilization cannot support two—or more—armed camps forever on the brink of nuclear catastrophe." Peace by terror or deterrent force in which belligerents threaten each other from week to week can lead only one place—to nuclear war.

A hunter of big game in Africa was getting close to his prey when, to his chagrin, his hard-pressed guides suddenly sat down to rest. He protested loudly, but to no avail. He threatened, pleaded, offered bribes—but the guides sat fanning under a tree. "But why," he implored the leader, "must you stop now?"

The guide answered with a wry smile. "Men say they have hurried so fast their bodies have run off and left their souls. Must wait for souls to catch up."

The breathless quest for power, wealth, influence and better technology has taken men—and nations—far into the jungle. Now, in this lag of culture and law, they need to pause for their souls to catch up. Nations are like children with guns in their hands. A child must be taught rules and laws; it would be unthinkable to send a six-year-old to school with a loaded rifle—but even a child understands why a policeman must carry a gun.

"It is impossible to imagine the heights to which may be carried, in a thousand years, the power of man over matter," wrote Benjamin Franklin. "O, that moral science were in as fair a way to improvement, that men would cease to be wolves to one another."

This is a gigantic arena for sacrifice—this imperative quest for a "break-through" in social science to match the achievements of technology. What matters it that men span the oceans at the speed of sound if, when they face their neighbors, they have nothing to say? Into this vacuum comes the missile or hydrogen war-head. Into this setting comes prejudice, ignorance, superstition—and tyranny. Man's pressing problems now are in the domain of the spirit —the "inner space" of human personality.

This new orientation toward the "inner man" demands the expenditure of greater resources and competence in the search for the deeper meanings of life. It means that research must be applied with equal vigor to man and machine—to the spiritual and the material. It means creating a new climate of adventure in human affairs to match the challenge of a rocket trip to outer space. It means that the quest for ways to link man to man and nation to nation must become as urgent as the quest to link earth with the moon.

Another area of sacrifice is the movement to get nations to put away their guns and solve their differences as law-abiding men. The goal is to seek an agreement between the arming nations to end the arms race—an undertaking far easier to propose than to accomplish. Who will sacrifice what? And what assurance can be given to disarming nations that other nations will fulfill their agreements? This opens up the Pandora's box of mutual inspection, the ability to detect, and the right to curtail the power of those who do not comply.

In a fable, the great beasts gather in the jungle to discuss disarmament. "Let us show our common enemy, man," said the lion, "how to live in peace together. If we set an example, perhaps he will cease to hunt and slay us."

"What do you propose?" inquired the bear.

The lion looked at the eagle. "Abolish wings," he suggested.

The eagle looked at the bull. "Destroy horns," he proposed.

The bull looked at the lion. "Get rid of teeth and claws," he demanded.

There was silence for a moment. All were staring at the bear. "I advise the elimination of all forms of defense," he said quietly. "In this way, each of you can have the security of my loving arms."

Any program of disarmament involves sacrifice. If great powers agree to disarm, they give up being great powers. No longer can they impress their views on other nations by threat of force. If they want to make sure that other nations are fulfilling their pledges, they, too, have to submit to measures of control. For some people, these concessions of authority and prestige are a deeply personal sacrifice. While other nations may welcome restraint of the great powers, feeling that their own stature is increased by removal of the threat of force, they may find that they have incurred increased responsibilities thereby. They may have to renounce a cherished neutrality and provide armed forces for the common defense. Disarmament may involve sacrifice also for the peoples of lesser powers.

Yet who would deny that such sacrifices are more than justified if they can help to prevent the horror of a third world war? The question is rather: are such sacrifices enough?

The answer is—no! In fact, the foregoing sacrifices become pure theory unless they are predicated upon a deeper and more significant kind of sacrifice—personal sacrifice. It is in the arena of individual, person-to-person relationships that true sacrifice begins. And it *must* begin here—and it must grow here, until the level of national leadership is raised and the vision of statesmen becomes the reflection of enlightened public opinion. Woodrow Wilson put it well: "The processes of liberty are that if I am your leader, you should talk to me, not that if I am your leader I should talk to you. I must listen, if I be true to the pledges of leadership, to the voices out of every hamlet, from every sort and condition of men."

Yet, the simple process of making one's voice heard is a sacrifice—more so in some places than in other, but there is bitter irony in the fact that in the places where it is easiest and most expected, it is a sacrifice too great to be endured. *Why should I bother? Who cares what I think, anyway? I'm too busy. The politicians make all the decisions.*

But the process of making one's voice a reasonable sound, based on knowledge, discussion, and insight is an even more challenging one. How much easier it is to get an "expert" to speak to the Rotary club than to dig into the facts and present the subject yourself? Granted a willingness to present it yourself, how much easier to give a lecture—your own opinions and your selection of facts—than to attempt to lead a spirited discussion in which a barrage of opinions may be laid down at you.

An into-their-shoes conference, previously mentioned, may take much time and study for several weeks on the part of the participants, but where one has been held it has raised the level of understanding of world affairs to an appreciable degree. If such study and debate were going on all around the world, who can estimate the values which could accrue? Yet, this illustrates that all such enterprises entail personal sacrifice of the hardest kind— the kind which steals from personal preoccupation with television-viewing, dancing lessons, parties, theatre-going, painting the basement, or building a boat.

Pericles said: "We do not allow absorption in our own affairs to interfere with participation in the city's; we yield to none in independence of spirit and complete self-reliance, but we regard him who holds aloof from public affairs as useless." And the Greeks had a word for the "useless" man, a "private" citizen, *idiotes,* from which the English word "idiot" comes.

This leads to another kind of personal sacrifice: the realization that our point of view may not be the right one, that the facts with which we are surrounded may be tainted with propaganda, that our culture may have something to learn from another culture. To many persons, this is the ultimate blow—the blow to personal and national pride. It is incredible to the superficial observer that the principles he has embraced, that the way of life he has ac-

76

cepted, may be almost unrecognizable in the next generation—that indeed its very base may be swept away and
society may possibly be the better for it.

This is a bitter dose to swallow, but such resiliency in
the human spirit may make the path of sacrifice much
easier to follow. With all the achievements of their civilization, the Greeks must have understood this well. For
thousands of years the trophy, or monument, has been the
symbol of victory, and these trophies have reflected in
their structure and substance the natural materials of the
land. In Egypt, where stone was plentiful, the monument
would be a slab or tablet engraved with the glorious record; farther east, it was sand, heaped high or in unusual
shapes, perhaps with severed heads or bones. In Greece
the substance was wood, out of which the victor might
form his trophy or monument. But it was not permitted to
be repaired! So, the victor always understood that it would
soon decay and rot away, even as he vanquished his foe
or as he erected his monument. The only permanent thing,
he well knew, was impermanence.

Such an attitude does not imply vacillation or lack of
objectives. It is not a peace-at-any-price doctrine, as the
record of the Greeks demonstrates. Such an attitude, however, creates perspective, and perspective is one of the
guideposts along the path of sacrifice.

The paths of justice and sacrifice merge here, but a discussion of attitudes which lead to sacrifice would be in-
complete without another reference to a foremost dilemma
of this atomic age. Even though the threat of annihilation
were abolished, another problem emerges laden with potential disaster. Misery and ignorance in the less developed
lands provide a paradise for the agitator, for the ambitious

individual, or for the nation seeking to gain power by fishing in troubled waters. Armed force cannot restrain the insurgent, for sooner or later he becomes armed. Yet, national disarmament and control of the great powers are of themselves no solution unless a new order can be established to encourage the hopes and win the allegiance of these emerging millions.

The crux of the matter here is: Who are these emerging millions? Ignorant savages who should be let alone? Potential laborers in a regimented technocracy? Soldiers marching in a bigger and more destructive army? Pawns in the game of power politics? Or, useful and free men who should somehow be helped to claim their rightful heritage of dignity, self-government, and self-respect. Each man will answer this question in his own way, but he will give his answer—even if it only is a decision not to answer at all.

The person drawn to the path of sacrifice will also take a fresh look at the meaning of *peace*. He will reflect about, and discuss, this word, probing for new meanings and new techniques. So long as the concept is negative and defined as "the absence of war," so long as effort is limited to restraining potential aggressors or curtailing the means of aggression, the results are likely to be disillusioning and dangerous. Only by transforming the concept to describe the positive and constructive task of creating order in the world can the individual discover a path which will justify his personal sacrifice.

The illiterate wrestling with his alphabet is waging peace. The agriculturist toiling to increase his yield, the men of science grappling with disease or patiently organizing ways to lessen the burdens of human toil, the businessman and the trade unionist raising standards of practice in their crafts, the individual citizens championing the cause of human rights or giving leadership in the development of international law—all these and many, many more are heroes in the quest for peace. The paths of freedom, progress, and justice, already commended to the Rotarian in the Outline of Policy, merge into the path of sacrifice—personal sacrifice for peace. And peace must be waged!

If international relations remain the preoccupation of demagogues and diplomats, the obstacles to peace may never be overcome. Peace must become the personal goal of practical men of affairs who are accustomed to getting things done. These men, if they will pause to consider the meaning of their lives, have the greatest stake of all in the issue. They have the most to lose in the present drift toward world war and revolution and the most to gain from the creation of a new order based on freedom, progress, and justice.

The path of sacrifice holds strong appeal for Rotarians. Truly, this is "Service Above Self." And thousands of Rotarians are responding. Much more could be accomplished, however, through a deeper devotion to Rotary principles, through a more diligent cultivation of Rotary contacts, and by more active and informed leadership in their own communities. Is this too much to expect from a "world fellowship of business and professional men united in the ideal of service"?

A generation ago, the fate of man was projected as "a race between education and catastrophe." With every year, the pace has quickened. The call for personal sacrifice grows more urgent. It comes from statesmen, scholars, and divines of every party and persuasion, but a general, long

79

exposed to the scenes of battle, has voiced the most categorical conviction:

> Now that the fighting has temporarily abated, the outstanding impression that emerges from the scene is the utter uselessness of the enormous sacrifice in life and limb which has resulted. A nation has been gutted and we stand today just where we stood before it all started.
>
> This experience again emphasizes the utter futility of modern war, its complete failure as an arbiter of international dissensions. We must finally come to realize that war is outmoded as an instrument of policy, that it provides no solution but international suicide.
>
> While we must be prepared to meet the trial if war comes, we should gear foreign and domestic policies toward the ultimate goal, the abolition of war from the face of the earth. You cannot control war; you can only abolish it.

It must be obvious that the abolition of war is a severe summons to sacrificial action. With a tenure so long in unrecorded tradition and in recorded history, and with a glory so enshrined in legend and song, it will die hard. But the trophies of a successful battle against this scourge of mankind make it worth the candle.

7

The Path of Loyalty

*He will urge and practice a spirit of under-
standing of every other man's beliefs as a step
towards international good will, recognizing
that there are certain basic moral and spiritual standards which, if practiced, will insure
a richer, fuller life.**

THE ROTARIAN who has seriously considered these paths
to peace might ask himself: "What more is needed?"

Surely these six paths—patriotism, conciliation, freedom,
progress, justice, and sacrifice—represent a catalogue of
courageous action tempered by vision. Here is a balanced
picture of an enlightened man:

— a patriot whose pride in the contributions of his beloved land rises above all assertions of national or
racial superiority;

* From the Outline of Policy in International Service.

— a stalwart defender of freedom for every human being;

— an optimist vigorous in support of action to improve
living standards;

— a realist determined to uphold justice by applying
its principles world-wide;

— a man prepared to make personal sacrifices for
peace.

What does he lack but the spiritual strength to sustain
him in this quest for peace?

This seventh path must involve the recognition that
man does not live by bread alone, that in this world of
competing ideologies, the cause of world fellowship must
reach beyond material considerations to encompass what
is of ultimate significance. Yes, this cause is practical; it
wrestles with such specific problems as prejudice, tension,
poverty, and injustice. But it must also be practical in the
most down-to-earth practicality of all—in giving point to
a man's life, and in seeking answers to the eternal questions: What is the meaning of it all? Why am I here?

Can Rotary propose such a path? If this seventh path
were to espouse any such teaching, it would be stepping
outside the function and sphere of Rotary. This fact can
hardly be stressed sufficiently. To dispel misconceptions,
it may suffice to quote the categorical reply of a president
of Rotary International to one great religious community
which raised the question:

Rotary is not a secret association. Rotary has no vows or
secrets of any kind. All of its meetings, activities, and records are public.

Rotary does not seek to supplant or to interfere with any
religious or charitable organization.

Many years ago, by convention action, Rotary International asserted: "Each Rotarian is expected to be a loyal member of the church or religious community to which he belongs and personally exemplify by his every act the tenets of his religion."

Qualifications for Rotary membership do not require information as to race, religion, or politics.

Rotary assumes that its program of service is in accord with all religions.

The key word in this statement is *loyal.* Each Rotarian is expected to be loyal to the religious community to which he belongs. And the Outline of Policy goes one step further by urging an understanding of the loyalties of other men as basic to the fulfillment of life's purpose. Unwillingness to understand persons with divergent loyalties is no small problem today. Rotary brings together men of different religious persuasions in a fellowship of mutual respect. Acquaintance in an atmosphere of mutual respect embraces a great deal. Given this setting, acquaintance ripens into friendship.

Project upon the world the simple ways of any Rotary club: the friendly greeting, the sitting down together, the exchange of experiences, the growing sympathy. Can this familiar process be developed between peoples now separated by barriers of suspicion, bitter memories, and differing loyalties? And could such world-wide acquaintance help heal the wounds of mankind? If it could, we might see realized the dream of the poet Whitman:

> I dreamed in a dream that I saw a city invincible to the attacks of the whole of the rest of the earth. I dreamed that was the new city of friends, the only city that will last, the only city that is impregnable, the new city of friends.

Much of the spiritual unrest which typifies industrialized society, and which, according to most authorities, is rapidly increasing, finds its origin in the pressures of society. The individual, floundering in events he does not understand or cannot control, looks inward. What does he see? He sees *other persons like himself*. And he discovers that his self-centered, self-sufficient being is only part of his reality. Behind his mask of selfishness is a truly spiritual being which is intimately concerned for, and linked with, other men and other women. This is the inner dynamism which reaches outward to others in the realization that, as Paul Tillich puts it, man is not "a thing among things"—he is a Person.

Ibsen in *Peer Gynt* has the superintendent of an insane asylum tell what is wrong with many of his patients. Those whom he described have psychopathic anxieties about themselves, not about others:

> Beside themselves? Oh, no, you're wrong. It's here that men are most themselves—Themselves and nothing but themselves—sailing with outspread wings of self, the cask stopped with the bung of self, and seasoned in a well of self. None has a tear for others' woes or cares what others think.

There is a universal "I" in humanity at its higher stages, and observers of social development see evidence that it reaches for, and interacts upon, others. The results of the "inner discovery" of Man may be gradual and at times uncertain, but they are unmistakable. There is a growing acknowledgment that if a person would serve himself, he must serve others. This fundamental truth is basic in Rotary.

Society being what it is, however, there is another side to the coin of such understanding. A canon of the Church

84

of England, renowned for his wit, once put the matter thus: "Today," he said, "we are all wild men, tired men, or puzzled men," as a result, he suggested, of the growth and spread of knowledge, of the corrosion of personal belief through association with other beliefs.

The attitudes and activities proposed for the path of loyalty are designed to guard against these corrosive effects of diversity. But first, perhaps, the effects themselves should be considered further. How, for example, does an individual respond to the discovery that others differ from him in belief? He may be one of the "wild men." When told that the world is gray, not black or white, he sees red. He regards the one who differs from him as a rival and an enemy. He resents his loyalty, burns his books, breaks up his assembly. He seeks to protect his own loyalty by isolating it; he relies on vehement and fanatical expressions; he may provoke his neighbors until they consent to make a martyr of him. He is the man who sees what he chooses to see and hears only what he wishes to hear. He is like the minister who, in making penciled notes in the margin of his sermon, wrote in one place: "Argument weak here— shout very loud."

A belligerent response to the discovery of diversity or unpleasant facts destroys the possibility of contribution along any of the paths commended to the Rotarian. No less destructive is the alternative response of the "tired men." Their interest and energy are sapped by the inability to decide for themselves. Like the "wild men," they demand a simple solution. Diversity distresses them, and often, tired of being tired, they make common cause with the fanatics. A great host of such weary souls are to be found in the train of any dictator. They may be among the

85

millions who have concluded that what they think does not matter, anyway—that "they" will make the decisions.

According to the canon, the remainder of mankind consists of the "puzzled men" who have neither isolated themselves in fanaticism nor surrendered to world weariness, yet who—confronted by many winds of doctrine—wonder what their answer should be to the eternal questions and how they are related to those who believe in other answers. They are forever gathering facts, searching out new "authorities," pondering new theories, and discussing the relevance of history; these are the persons who defer action or commitment until "all the facts are in." Consequently, their decisions, such as they are, are "decisions by default."

For the "puzzled men" the path of loyalty provides an answer which can rescue them from the state of suspended judgment. Loyalty means commitment and action; commitment to something larger than oneself, and beyond oneself. It means "digging in" at a logical point and saying: "Here I take my stand. From here, I can go on exploring. But as of now I stand here with my fellow men!" It involves others who share the same devotion—"the dear love of man for his comrade," as Whitman called it. For the "tired men" the path of loyalty is presented as a delight and an encouragement to living. Come what may, there is something that the loyal person can harvest home: the challenge of the probing spirit, the thrill of creative service, the solid anchor of personal responsibility. It is normal that men should look for easy methods—the down-hill paths, the ready-made solutions. In a push-button, free-wheeling age, it is natural that men should look for Instant Loyalty, Instant Peace. If there can be Instant War, the others should be available, too. But they are not here.

A fable illustrates the ultimate tragedy of the "tired man" —the person who, from weariness or from laziness, concludes that one man's contribution will never be missed, anyway. It was decided that all the people on earth would shout "Boo!" at the same time so that the voice of the world would be heard on the moon. When the moment came for the mighty shout, all the people were so eager to hear this loud noise that each person decided to listen and not contribute his "Boo!" It was said that this great occasion passed as the most silent moment in all history.

To the "wild men" it must be said that others are inspired to see one who knows where he is going—yet one who rejoices in encounters with loyalties different in object and origin from his own. Knowing and appreciating the depths of their devotions, his own allegiance gathers fervor, just as travelers who chance to meet in their journeys are cheered on their several ways. Acquaintance, the heart of Rotary, is also an act of the imagination— a projection of the soul into the soul of another human being, or of several others, or of a whole people.

Rotary is designed to amplify and multiply this process for the advancement of understanding, good will, and peace: intensively in the club—men of different occupations and different faiths are brought together; extensively —through the world fellowship of Rotary—each member has the chance to inspire and be inspired by men of other nations, cultures, and traditions. One man's witness to the meaning of life strengthens the sense of meaning in others.

At many points along the line, however, loyalty has been discredited. How else can be explained the apathy toward religion, as distinguished from mere church-going, the weakening of family attachments, the number of broken homes, the rash of treason to country which has been revealed even among persons of the finest backgrounds and privileges, the wild fanaticism and the listless emptiness of so many lives? Many reasons, social and economic, can be advanced for these developments, but would they have occurred if the training in loyalty had not been neglected or cheapened? One disillusioned writer put his experience this way: "I was part of that strange race of people aptly described as spending their lives doing things they detest, to make money they don't want, to buy things they don't need, to impress people they don't like." What a picture of futility—the absence of any loyalty to anything or to anybody!

To the Prince of Darkness exulting on his throne, the story goes, came one who whispered evil tidings. Somewhere on the earth, man had discovered a good idea. For a moment, Satan was abashed and shaken, but he soon recovered and with a devilish grin replied:

"Never mind, I will teach them how to organize it."

Throughout the world are countless manifestations of the tendency to cheapen good ideas, to organize the heart out of them, to dilute them with words and trappings until they have no meaning. Even the natural impulse of children to group themselves in pursuit of an interest is routinized and exploited. Athletics, which provide such wonderful training in the team spirit, is often corrupted by emphasis on star performance and box office receipts. Sublime moments in the year consecrated to religious and patriotic devotions have been perverted to base purposes.

Around the world in many places, loyalty has been perverted on a grand scale, because it serves immediate ends—without any regard for whom or what may be sacrificed in the process. In such a setting, a Way of Life becomes an obsession, a scheme of economics becomes a religion, words become realities. The ongoing search for Truth becomes not a discovery through observation or experience but a quest for facts which confirm pre-conceived axioms. Regimentation and totalitarianism reach into the mind and lock the gate against Truth. In totalitarian countries, loyalty is always under direct attack. Children are trained to spy on their parents and teachers. Ideas are strictly censored lest loyalty to truth and justice question the aims of the State. Fear of guilt by association discourages personal friendships. Independent groupings for social, religious, or political purposes are subjected to persecution.

Yet, despite all these depressing circumstances, the impulse to loyalty refuses to be crushed. Under the fire of martyrdom, it burns brighter and purer. Even the terrors of the concentration camp and the sacrifice of security have not prevented hundreds of thousands from breaking out for refuge in those parts of the world where voluntary loyalty is still possible.

The heroic motives of those who risk much for freedom, however, should not be misunderstood. A pertinent comment came from the young Polish flyer who deserted his homeland to bring out the first Russian jet plane the West had seen, except in combat. A few weeks later a reward of $100,000 was offered to any MIG pilot who would emulate his feat. The response was disappointing, and the Polish pilot was asked for an explanation. He suggested that those likely to take the risk would be prompted by honor and love of freedom, not by hope of gain. Loyalty cannot be purchased.

But the press of materialism has made inroads against

loyalty. The whole world is rushing toward the creation
or accumulation of things. Nations vie with each other in
steel production, in car loadings, and in manufacturing.
The symbol of a successful society is not the great ideas
or great men it creates, but the *things* it produces. And
things have their place in the process of emancipating mankind from toil, privation, and drudgery, but emancipated
for what?

It is a picture typified by a man and wife making a long
journey by automobile. The wife was reading the map and
giving directions. Suddenly, the wife exclaimed, "John,
we're lost."

The husband clenched the wheel, pushed the accelerator
even harder, and said, "What's the difference—we're making wonderful time!"

Mankind lives in an age of technology, with machines
harnessed to almost every facet of life—even to the thought
processes. The "march of progress" has become the end, not
the means; the destination of life is of little consequence.
It is not surprising that men tend to emphasize action
rather than thought, things rather than persons, progress
rather than loyalty. Materialism without the tempering of
loyalty leads inevitably to the attitude which says: *There
is no future, there is no past, there's only now.*

Observing how loyalty has been cheapened and suppressed, some might conclude that loyalty is a lost cause.
But appearances are often mistaken for reality. Time and
again through history, causes that seemed to be lost inspired the heights of loyalty. The strength of loyalty is not
manifested in applause for the conqueror or in mounting
the triumphant bandwagon, but rather in the moments of
utter despair. Consider the Christian martyrs braving the

90

might of Rome. Think of the patriots who sustained their loyalty through centuries when their countries had been wiped from the map.

The richest personal experiences, too, may come at the time when the presence of loyalty is most keenly felt. Are not these the times of trial and faint hope?

The statesman who exemplified the stubborn will of a nation standing alone against impossible odds voiced a confidence that subsequent events have made more plausible. "Laws just or unjust may govern men's actions," Sir Winston Churchill told an American audience in 1949. "Tyrannies may restrain or regulate their words. The machinery of propaganda may pack their minds with falsehood and deny them truth for many generations of time. But the soul of man thus held in trance or frozen in a long night can be awakened by a spark coming from God knows where, and in a moment the whole structure of lies and oppression is on trial for its life. People in bondage need never despair."

Many spectacular headlines are created by men who suppress freedom, embrace selfish goals, and exalt brute strength—those whose loyalty, such as it is, remains in the cave-man stage. Their narrow causes, gnawing at the spirit of men, are still taking their toll, but the human spirit springs back if it is nurtured and inspired by steadfast loyalty. Rotary's appeal has been to the loyalty of men— to the selfless spirit reaching out to the same spirit in other men. Patriotism, conciliation, freedom, progress, justice, and sacrifice—each of these represents a counsel of perfection which is hard to achieve, but Rotarians possess a deep feeling of loyalty to a world fellowship which links them with all people. Theirs is an expansive loyalty, but grounded well on foundations which have withstood the tides and currents of their communities.

Loyalty belongs to what has been called the "unyielding frontier" of the human spirit, which will not submit to laboratory or test-tube. Scientists can shrink the world to one geographic neighborhood, but they cannot make the neighbors like or respect one another. They can neither isolate nor create motives which can be applied automatically to produce respect and service in an interdependent world. Research geniuses are more likely to produce life than to create *love*. The last word belongs to the spirit.

A scientist, however, speaking to a Rotary International convention, sketched a passage out of the Valley of Imminent Destruction—a passage which can demonstrate how a blending of the path of progress and the path of loyalty could lead to peace. Dr. Donald H. Andrews, a chemist, told the Rotarians and their families:

> The same experiments which have given us atomic energy are giving us . . . atomic vision. We are looking inside the atom and we are seeing that the atom is more than matter. If you want it in a word, we are seeing that the atom is music. And it is because of this new vision, the fact that science points to something beyond the material, we can find hope for the future, hope that we can at last build this great, new, wonderful world of peace and abundant living for everyone. . . .
>
> What is this mysterious force within each of us that dominates and controls this vast flux of atoms that goes through us in every moment of our living? Science today asserts that the quantity which stays constant under transformation has the deepest reality.
>
> Here is this life spark, call it spirit or soul, if you like, which somehow within us *stays* constant and dominates

this vast change, that constitutes our living, and there we have the supreme reality. Science says the reality which we know and with which we have contact, the supreme dominant reality, is the human spirit. Now, if we turn to the universe without as well as the universe within, we find the same answer. The stars are made of atoms. Their atoms are singing. The music of the spheres is more than just a poet's fancy. The stars are singing. And, as we look further out at the nature of time and space, we see again a new answer. . . .

The real power of the universe is not the shattering power of the atom but the power of love, the love that we should have for our fellow human beings, the love which our Creator has for us and which we should have for Him. And in terms of these new visions of science we see hope for bringing in this new world of peace, good will, and abundant living for all mankind. . . .

Rotarians can provide no instant magic in bringing in this new world, but they are in an enviable position to engage in a "chain reaction" of fellowship and service. One Rotarian—like the process of the exploding atom—can be the catalyst for two; those two can touch off four; four can reach eight—and so on. They can have such faith and vision that their loyalties can ignite others with the same vision.

Rotary has no quick solution to offer a harried world, but Rotarians—individual Rotarians—believe they have widened the crack in the wall of misunderstanding and distrust. With every passing day they hasten its disintegration by a barrage of fellowship and service. They do not toil alone, and they take courage that all men of good will are joined, in spirit, in the universal quest for peace.

Impact

SHORTLY BEFORE an election, the London borough of Lambeth organized an exhibition to encourage voters to exercise their privilege on election day. There were all sorts of interesting features; picturesque episodes in the long struggle for the right to vote, charts showing the ebb and flow of voter interest in past elections, maps and models of new developments planned for the borough with brief biographies of the candidates. But most magnetic of all the attractions was a mysterious box. It bore a sign reading:

THIS PERSON CARRIES THE HEAVIEST BURDEN.

Visitors were invited to peer within and to press a button. A light went on disclosing the only contents of the box—a looking glass!

If a Rotary club were to hold an exhibition of international service, might not the very same feature be included? A mirror for the individual Rotarian to look at himself! It would dramatize the thought of the international service committee of a Rotary club in Denmark at the end of a splendid year's work:

The international work must be carried out by every single member of the club. The international service committee is not a separate, sole agency or department within the club. The committee directs, advises, informs and assists you, the individual member, in all matters pertaining to international service in order that you may do your part in this essential Rotary service. As a Rotarian it is YOUR responsibility.

This thought was the basis of the program of one president of Rotary International who challenged individual Rotarians to find their "personal paths to peace." This admonition creates an obligation to set personal objectives, to survey every facet of the local scene to find where service and information may be helpful. This is not to dictate to the individual Rotarian but to help him to do what he wants to do, what he knows he should do, and to persuade him that what he does is important. It should be clearly understood by Rotarians and non-Rotarians, too, that the *impact* of Rotary is created by individual Rotarians.

"After years of concentrated effort," writes the New Zealand Rotarian who initiated the study of the seven paths to peace, "the central problem remains the same. We are still trying to devise ways and means of capturing the imagination of the individual Rotarian. Opportunity is there, information is there, the desire to use both is there in the majority of members. Yet we still have to persuade the individual that his effort, however small, will and does affect the total."

What *can* the Rotarian do? What has he already done? What opportunities come to the Rotarian because he is a Rotarian? And has he taken advantage of these opportunities? These are only a few of the searching questions which will come to the Rotarian—and the non-Rotarian too—as he reads the story of other Rotarians and, more important, as he appraises his own movements along his "personal path to peace."

First, it should be pointed out that *being* a Rotarian sets up advantages and opportunities not presented to many persons. The Rotarian can open his Official Directory of more than 10,000 clubs in more than 100 lands, turn to any page, put his finger down on a club listing and say, "Here I have a friend." He can write a personal letter to that club president or secretary with the expectation of getting a personal reply. He can visit that club on a meeting day and be welcomed as a *friend*. He may be a guest in any Rotarian's place of business or in his home. The candor—and respect—with which Rotarians approach each other is significant.

Rotarians travel a great deal. In these days when no point on the earth is more than a few hours away, travel to other lands is easy and attractive. Thousands of Rotarians travel in other countries each year, and the number is increasing. "Making up" in another club is not only a necessity, it is a privilege which no Rotarian would forego.

Imagine the experience of such a traveler. Before his departure, the traveling Rotarian is urged by his fellow Rotarians to visit as many Rotary clubs as possible in his journey. He may be given the simulated "passport" available from Rotary International, as a reminder of the meeting places and times of the clubs he might visit. Over the endorsement of his club officers, it authorizes him to invite the co-operation of the clubs in international service.

When he goes into the meeting of a club in another country, he goes not as stranger or "foreigner" but as fellow-Rotarian. His conversation with neighbors at lunch, the brief remarks he may be asked to make, and the message of good will he brings from his own club are impressive. They will be remembered, especially if he is visiting a club in a smaller or more remote community. And that is not all. He may be invited to the home of a member or to his place of business. An interview may appear in the local newspaper or be broadcast over the radio. He may be taken to the school for a talk about his country.

Many Rotary clubs, because of their location near international borders, can regularly sponsor personal, face-to-face meetings with other Rotarians. Ill-will between nations is often generated by border incidents. Rotarians so located—and there are many—have a special responsibility for insuring that incidents are of the kind to foster international good will.

It can be done. It is being done all the time. Here, an international peace park bestrides a frontier as a result of Rotary sponsorship; there, a great meeting brings hundreds of Rotarians from the neighbor country year after year. School children exchange visits from country to country under Rotary guidance. Airplanes are chartered to fly the whole club to another country for an inter-city meeting. The famous statue of Christ, dedicated by Rotarians of Argentina and Chile to enduring peace, towers in the highest Andes. All kinds of exchanges are fostered by the Inter-Country Committees that carry on a continuous activity in Europe. And from India comes this note of a Rotary mission to Pakistan:

> Nearly 200 Rotarians from every city and town of note, representing the chivalry of Rajastan, the shrewdness of Sarastra, the business and industry of Gujarat, and the past memories of Central India wended their way to Karachi on a mission of Rotary and as ambassadors of peace and good will.

If border incidents of this kind could be multiplied, if every Rotarian who travels would undertake a Rotary mission for his club, a great advance in understanding and good will could be achieved.

"Meet thy neighbor, talk with him, and there will be peace."

An Indian Rotarian writes of this old Sanskrit proverb: "Simple language, but wonderful wealth of meaning behind it. There is, I think, not only a challenge to Rotary, but I feel that Rotary is the best equipped vehicle in the world to achieve this prime purpose of civilization."

Not all Rotarians can journey to another land, but most of them can be hosts to those who can, or, what may be more practical, they can use the mails for fruitful and stimulating exchange. Personal acquaintance through international correspondence, as in all phases of Rotary, is not developed as an end in itself, delightful as that is, but "as an opportunity for service." What that opportunity may be is a matter for exploration with correspondents. In one instance, there may be a contribution to better understanding of a particularly troublesome problem. In another, the exchange of books and magazines for presentation to local libraries may be the result. Or, hearing about some effort of the other club for the welfare of its community, the Rotarian may be inspired to offer help, too. The possibilities are as infinitely varied as the needs of mankind.

Where to begin? That is the question! One Rotarian in Norway found an answer by treating himself to a world tour—addressing letters in sequence to one Rotary club after another in progression around the world. What a reception he got en route! There may be some special interest, professional or otherwise, that would lead to the choosing of a particular country as the starting point of a quest for understanding. Perhaps there is hostility toward a certain country manifested in casual conversation with a neighbor or in the remarks of a newspaper columnist or radio commentator. Why not write to Rotarians in that country with a tactful request for enlightenment?

In that event, the following statement of policy should be given close attention:

> The board of directors of Rotary International shares with Rotarians everywhere deep concern over tense and troubled conditions in many parts of the world; great satisfaction in the services rendered by Rotary clubs, Rotarians and many others in relieving distress; and a clear recognition of the urgent need for understanding and good will among the peoples of the world.
>
> The board has earnestly sought and will continue to seek every means, within the limits of established policy, to attain the objectives of Rotary International throughout the world.
>
> The board has reviewed statements and activities of some Rotary clubs which, however well intended, in some instances have resulted in misunderstanding, ill will, and controversy.
>
> The board urges all Rotary clubs and Rotarians to intensify their efforts to encourage and foster the advancement of understanding and good will among the peoples of the world—at all times observing established policy of Rotary International and avoiding scrupulously any act, utterance, correspondence or published statement which might have a tendency to cause misunderstanding, create ill will, or retard efforts to achieve and maintain peace.

Individual Rotarians around the world have derived rare

satisfaction from correspondence on a grand scale. A Brazilian supported the cause of international understanding with 6,000 personal letters. A Rotary club in Hawaii bases the discussions of its international service committee on correspondence by its members. A Texan reports the writing of 12,000 letters with a view to promoting correspondence between young people of different countries. As one Canadian Rotarian, who was carrying on a lively exchange with 38 friends in Rotary overseas, exclaimed: "Why don't more Rotarians start writing letters? It is no hardship and, I can assure you, very enjoyable. I can hardly wait until I get my next letter from some previously unheard from overseas club."

More than 1,500 Rotary clubs in some 60 countries have registered their interests in the publication, "Targets for Today," published annually and brought up to date at least once within the year with a supplement. If you are initiating correspondence, you may want to select one of those "target" clubs.

One outgrowth of correspondence may be an exchange of manuscripts, recordings, films, or slides. This practice is a favorite program technique of hundreds of clubs. The best talent of each club is enlisted for the exchange program, and direct references are often made to personalities in the other club to emphasize the feeling of fellowship. When the program from the other club is presented at a regular meeting it is introduced impressively as a notable occasion of Rotary in action. If the exchange program is in manuscript, members reading it assume the parts of the original spokesmen and are introduced as such with brief biographies. The other country's flag is displayed, its national anthem played, and a toast proposed.

Local residents of that country are honored guests at the meeting and press reports of it are sent to the originating club.

Electronic magic can reproduce for Rotarians of another country the actual talk and other sounds of the club meeting. Movies or slides can bring vivid impressions of Rotary personalities and scenes in other lands. Hundreds of clubs have combined slides and recordings to make impressive and stimulating programs.

The obstacle of a different language cannot be dismissed, but it can be overcome. In many cases, the language will be understood by someone in the other club who can translate correspondence or an exchange program in manuscript for the benefit of other members. At the beginning of a correspondence, the language situation should be clarified so that each party to the exchange can feel free to use his own language.

The fruits of personal acquaintance between Rotarians of different countries may seem small in contrast with the immensity of the issues that harass the world. Greater, then, is the need to multiply and intensify these contacts. The Rotarian will not be content with one letter or one exchange of programs. He will initiate many. He will use the wonders of science to expedite his originality. Stretching out his hands in many directions, persevering with acquaintance once established, he can develop an influence that will spread over the earth.·

Turning from the personal activities of Rotarians within their own ranks, what can they do to reach non-Rotarians? Or, should they?

The answer is—yes! A Rotarian represents a single business or profession—the only representative of that business or profession in his club. His obligation to carry the Rotary ideal of service to others of his profession or business as well as to the community at large is a primary concern. He will find his "personal path to peace," but more will be accomplished if he can convince others to travel it with him.

A significant part of the impact of Rotary, then, is the extent of its influence beyond the Rotary club itself. It is obvious that the object of Rotary can hardly be achieved if this influence is limited to the relatively small number of Rotarians. This imperative was plainly drawn by the founder of Rotary. "In the promotion of international understanding and good will," wrote Paul Harris, "one must remember that it is important to reach large numbers, non-Rotarians as well as Rotarians, and one cannot reach large numbers privately."

Rotarians, accordingly, are challenged to open a window to the world for the people of their communities. Here, indeed, is an answer to those who question the practical effects of international service. International understanding will not be created in the stratosphere of world politics —but in the minds of neighbors, among business associates, and through local media of communication and education. Public opinion is the sum of individual opinions, and public opinion is the mightiest force on earth. Nations are as strong as the sum of individual opinions that can be mobilized in support of their policies.

Legislators and government officials are frank to admit that a single letter bearing the marks of simple sincerity and individual inspiration has more weight with them than reams of stereotyped petitions. A forthright remark in casual conversation can have profound repercussions.

In the Senate of the United States there sat for many years a Rotarian, the late Senator Charles Andrews, Florida, U.S.A., who spoke out strongly for international understanding. He liked to tell his friends that he remembered his Rotary training whenever international relations were discussed. Asked how he got that training, he would say that it might have come from speeches on international service, but mostly it came from the table talk at the club meeting where he learned the individual sentiments of his fellow members. Little they knew the consequence of their casual comments in the preparation of a statesman.

Programs presented at weekly meetings are an excellent opportunity for sharing with non-Rotarians. Because of the scope and program of Rotary, no club can be excused for having weekly programs "just like any other club." Programs with an international service theme will be planned around the needs of the community. The needs vary, of course, from place to place. A long look at one town may disclose deep-seated prejudices against "foreigners." Many a Rotary club has derived satisfaction from a program that calls attention to the debt that every nation owes to the culture, the art, the science of other nations. In the progress of mankind all nations are members one of another. The same is true in mundane matters of raw materials, manufactured products, and markets. Do people recognize the extent of this interdependence? Is the worker who eats his breakfast and rides off to his work aware that neither of these functions, nor many others that fill his day, would be possible without material contributions from lands other than his own?

The interest of any community in this fact of interdependence can be aroused by an exhibit that displays the best contributions of other countries. Often these contributions are already present, yet unsuspected by most of the people. A prairie town in Canada was astonished when the Rotary club arranged a folk festival—many different nationalities were represented—and an abundance of talent was displayed. Treasured costumes, folk songs and dances, souvenirs of many kinds which had been brought from other countries—all combined to transform a rather drab community into a veritable Ali Baba's cave of cosmopolitan culture.

Other needs may relate to particular problems. What, for instance, are the attitudes toward the overwhelming issue of war or peace—hopeful, constructive, and determined in the search for positive solutions? Or resentful, fearful, and impatient—ripe for the mob hysteria that drives nations to convulsions of despair?

What can the Rotary club do to allay fears, encourage the acquiring of information, and create a climate where freedom and justice are secure? Perhaps nothing. But clubs have done such things and are doing them every day. Such projects go beyond "having a program about it"—a weekly program which can only deal briefly and superficially with the subject. Here, a *program* means a sustained and organized campaign in which the weekly program is merely one of the tools.

Fortunately, Rotary is not without allies for these tasks. In every community there are individuals and groups with similar purposes and with special spheres of influence whose co-operation can be sought. Rotary projects of international service can well be guided in this respect by the policy of co-operating with an existing agency, if one exists, rather than to create a new and duplicative agency.

Instances of the operation of this principle in international service abound. Perhaps the most spectacular was that initiated in 1942 by Rotarians of the London (England) area in organizing a conference of 21 governments to discuss cultural exchange after the war. That conference became in due course the United Nations Educational, Scientific, and Cultural Organization, more familiarly known as UNESCO, an independent agency pursuing the goals of international understanding.

Under somewhat analogous circumstances, the president of Rotary International was invited to appoint 11 United States Rotarians who, in turn, were invited to advise the United States delegation at the San Francisco conference where the United Nations charter was negotiated.

While Rotary International is recognized as a consultant by the United Nations and UNESCO, this fact in no way identifies Rotary with these organizations. The position was clearly set forth in the following statement by the board of directors of R.I. in January, 1952:

> While R.I. neither gives nor withholds endorsement of the United Nations charter, nor of the actions or enactments of the United Nations, it does encourage Rotarians to acquaint themselves with the activities of the United Nations directed to the advancement of world peace.

> The general secretary is instructed to bring to the attention of Rotary clubs program information and other helps in connection with the study of the charter and the activities of the United Nations to the advancement of world peace.

> Continued publicity shall be given to the reports of observers for R.I. who attend meetings of the United Nations and its specialized agencies.

> Rotarians desiring to make a proposal concerning the United Nations or any of its specialized agencies should

function through the duly constituted governmental chan-
nels of their own country.

Many Rotarians around the world are active in the work
of their local United Nations Associations. Many local
chapters were founded as a result of the initiative of Rotarians.

An example—one of many—of an enterprise initially
sponsored by Rotary clubs which evolved into community-
sponsored projects is the Institutes for International Understanding. For thirteen years, an annual audience of
more than a million non-Rotarians heard speakers—many
of them from other countries—discuss world problems, answer questions, and meet with the assemblies of local
schools. Through these meetings, hundreds of Rotary clubs
were able to reach large numbers, and eventually many
communities sponsored them on their own.

How a Rotary club can co-operate with many other
agencies in a community to meet a need not being met by
any one of them has been illustrated in an entirely novel
way in several communities. Adult citizens of the community in which it began in 1957 were organized in delega-
tions representing many nations in an into-their-shoes conference. This technique, which has been cited previously,
offers promise of being an appealing and effective method
for attracting "large numbers" to international service.
Here is *impact* at its best.

For a full month, the "delegates" debate major world
problems. The active interest of hundreds of participants,
putting themselves "into the shoes" of a nation other than
their own, is amazing. It spills over from the prescribed
committee and plenary sessions into countless private gath-

erings and conversations that seek to win support for rec-
ommendations. Here is active self-education, replacing the
passive indoctrination by pressure groups. Most significant
of all perhaps is the personal acquaintance developed
among people representing widely different views.

Does this experience provide a pattern that Rotary clubs
around the world can adapt to their purposes? All that is
needed is the initial impetus.

Turning to the leaders of tomorrow, there is no end to
ways in which Rotary clubs, with their world-wide affilia-
tions, can contribute to the education of the rising generation. Sponsoring an international relations club is a common practice. Pen friendships are arranged for youth
through Rotary clubs abroad. Japanese clubs, for instance,
have excited wide interest with an exchange of drawings
by school children. International essay contests to promote
a better understanding are often a joint project undertaken
by the Rotary clubs in different countries.

Without interfering in any sense with the curriculum of
the schools, teachers or administrators might be asked to
tell the Rotary club how children are being informed about
their world. Is the approach universal or provincial, as illustrated in the story told by a former American ambassador to India? His son, fresh from Asian experiences, was
about to enter an American school.

"I'll make a bet," said the ambassador, "that the world
history which you will study begins in Egypt and Meso-
potamia, moves on to Greece by way of Crete, takes you
through Rome and finally ends with France and England."

"But that is not *world* history," argued his son. "That
leaves out three-fourths of the world."

"Unfortunately," the father remarks, "I won the bet."

The exchange of youth has offered the greatest challenge to Rotary clubs. In this field Rotary has pioneered with countless club and district sponsorships of various types of exchange and with the Rotary Foundation Fellowships which began in 1947.

The promise inherent in the Rotary Foundation program has appealed to Rotarians around the world. More than 1,200 graduate students have studied in countries other than their own, under Rotary sponsorship. Incidents culled from their reports and from the comments of others could fill volumes. Each year they address audiences totalling more than half a million. Even more minds are reached by radio and through articles they write for many publications. And of no less significance are the evidences of character and ability reflected in their activities. Truly, they are among tomorrow's leaders.

One feature makes the Rotary Foundation Fellowships program unique: the degree of personal interest, friendship, and guidance that is forthcoming from Rotarians who "host" them in their academic communities, who take them into their homes and show them truly how the community works. Not all Rotarians avail themselves of this unique opportunity for helping to train future leaders, but most of them do.

Rotarians will derive a dividend from their investments in The Rotary Foundation to the extent that they take advantage of the opportunity to use the capacities and influence the thinking of these potential ambassadors of good will. Many Fellows have expressed their feelings about this opportunity, but it was never more charmingly set forth than by a young lady addressing one of the clubs in Australia:

In San Francisco it has been jokingly said that when they built the Golden Gate bridge, a thread was tied round a pigeon's leg. The pigeon flew across the bay and when he reached the other side a heavy cord was tied on to the string and pulled across. After the cord they pulled a small cable and then a still heavier one until finally the cable that holds the Golden Gate bridge was strung across.

I like to think that the Rotary Foundation Fellowships are a bit like that. They are the thread that will mark increasing exchanges between students of all countries who desire a deeper understanding of each other. It is just a thread now, but each year it is growing stronger and stronger. Next year perhaps it will be a rope, and finally it must be a big cable bridging the gap between the nations and binding us all together in a peaceful world. I am proud and grateful for the privilege of being part of this great movement in furthering international understanding.

Rotary clubs have not only contributed generously to The Rotary Foundation but also they have used their own resources and ingenuity to set up and sponsor their own exchange of youth. While The Rotary Foundation has sponsored the exchange of graduate students, the great preponderance of club and district projects have involved undergraduate or secondary students. The study and travel of more than 10,000 young persons are sponsored by clubs and districts each year!

One such project has been in continuous operation since 1944, and its sponsors comment, "Our only regret is that we did not start something of this kind 25 years ago." Another district project which has brought nearly 300 students to America from a score of countries involves joint sponsorship by the district and individual clubs. A principal advantage claimed for this plan is the intense interest developed by these clubs in their "own" students.

Increasingly, individual clubs are discovering that the sponsoring of visits by youth from abroad is well within their capacity. These plans put personal service ahead of purse service. The youth is lodged in the homes of Rotarians. The local school, in many instances, is happy to provide free tuition for the sake of the cosmopolitan influence, and the offer of such an opportunity enables Rotary clubs of other lands to select a fine representative youth from many applicants who are eager and able to pay their own travel expenses. Thereby, the cost of such projects to the sponsoring clubs is limited to incidentals. One club brought 11 students from nine countries for a year to its community.

In Europe, youth exchange is a well-established practice. Rotary district governors appoint committees to make the arrangements. Often the exchange involves only the cost of travel. The experience of home life in another country, the opportunity to learn another language, and the cementing of Rotary fellowship across national boundaries are only a few of the benefits. International tours and summer camps have multiplied in Europe. One example of how they are appreciated is the story of the Austrian lad who rode his bicycle all the way to Holland to join an international cruise aboard a Dutch vessel.

The instrument of personal acquaintance works most effectively in these summer camps. As one German boy wrote of his experience:

> This camp has done more for international understanding than a big number of politicians could do in a year. If there is a possibility to form a united Europe, then it can only be done when all the different nations will be able to

overcome their prejudices. I am sure that the Rotary club camp really was successful in overcoming these prejudices, and that this is not all an exaggeration of mine.

When all is said and done, the personal touch is what counts in these international student projects. Hordes of young people are shuttled across the seven seas in vain if no effort is made to train them for international service.

While the Rotary Foundation Fellowships and other Rotary-sponsored visits provide a natural focus for this effort, there is a broader field in the thousands of students and trainees going abroad each year under other schemes or on their own often slender resources. Many of them seldom see much of the country they visit, or its people. Among the thousands of such visitors to the U.S.A. in a year, it is estimated that 80 per cent never see the inside of an American home. Probably the situation is not much different in other lands.

The importance of building friendships in this way becomes evident when it is remembered how many national leaders—how many Nehrus, how many Nkrumahs and others—once lived abroad. If they experienced isolation, loneliness, and discrimination, the world could suffer deeply from those wounds. A Mexican statesman who made great contributions to international understanding recalls the years of loneliness spent in a hall bedroom in New York City. Only the kindness of some neighbors in the tenement rescued him from a feeling of bitterness which might have warped his whole career.

The Rotarian who introduces a visiting student to normal home life and to his neighbors, shows him how business is done, and shares with him the simple pleasures of everyday life is not only making a friend for himself—he may be doing his country and the world a great service. His discussions of world problems with the youth may bear fruit in a career of leadership in the cause of peace.

But the greatest challenge, of course, is to those Rotary clubs in the neighborhood of universities. Theirs is a continuous and developing opportunity to organize acquaintance with students from abroad. Rotarians meet these opportunities well and wisely. Students by the hundreds are entertained during holiday seasons; churches and schools call upon them to interpret their countries in song and story; individuals are generous in their financial and spiritual solicitude. Admitting all this with pride, however, does not minimize the necessity of doing more!

Doing more in all activities reflected in the "looking glass" becomes a personal challenge to the Rotarian who reads his official magazine and other Rotary publications. In an organization of the scope and size of Rotary, communication is basic. To know what others are doing, to understand how they did it—this becomes a challenge and an inspiration, for if the idea became reality in Hyderabad, it might have appeal in Huntsville.

Rotary's growth and success, after all, have come from the leavening of the spirit of service, and every success story speaks boldly, "You can do this, too—and better." And in the processes of communication and inspiration Rotary's official magazine—*The Rotarian* in English and *Revista Rotaria* in Spanish—makes the major impact. Twenty-two regional magazines also make impact in their limited spheres.

Rotary publications present facts and reflect ideas which have more than Rotary appeal. Hundreds of copies of Rotary books, magazines, and pamphlets are shared with non-

Rotarians around the world. When these publications find their way into almost a half million homes of Rotarians, they have just begun their journey.

The magazine, for example, goes in large numbers to schools, public libraries, hospitals, reading rooms, and in hundreds of other places where accurate, readable, and constructive reporting is highly valued. Its articles are the bases for excellent Rotary club programs, for women's social and study club programs, and for young people's discussion groups. It provides references for educational reports in schools and colleges, and radio and television programs are based on its articles.

Beyond these uses, however, in its two editions it is the "textbook," or a vital supplement to the textbook, in hundreds of classes where students are learning a new language. Its impact is enhanced by its being the only such magazine indexed by the *Reader's Guide to Periodical Literature*, and its influence is attested to by thousands of article reprints which are requested by Rotarians and non-Rotarians alike.

These, then, have been some of the images reflected in the looking glass—several of the acts of service which enrich the life of the individual Rotarian. No person, no publication, could chronicle all of them. No one can even cite examples of all of them. The nature of Rotary itself and the nature of the Rotarians who make up this organization make the gathering of stories of service very difficult. The service of Rotarians is likely to be quiet service. And this is as it should be.

International service in Rotary is not the sound of trumpets. It heralds no pronouncements. It seeks no headlines. Accordingly, this book has merely set forth, developed, and illustrated several of the principles in which Rotarians believe and around which they take their stand, as individual citizens. The result of more than a half century of successful experience, these principles may be worth consideration by persons who do not belong to Rotary clubs. For Rotary neither holds their exclusive possession nor claims their original creation.

An "international walk" graces the broad plaza leading to the headquarters building of Rotary International. From the marble quarries that yielded stone for the Parthenon, from the floor of Westminster Abbey, from cliffs two miles above the sea in the Peruvian Andes—from most of the lands where Rotary is at work have come its square-cut paving stones.

They form a colorful pattern: red from Australia, yellow from France, dark gray from Singapore, cherry-pink from Japan, bird-blue from Sweden. To withstand the strains of climate, only the most durable stones were selected, and embedded in each is a metal plaque telling the country, the year of Rotary's arrival, and the name of its first club.

Joined together in common service, these stones are silent but enduring witness to Rotary's methods and goals. They symbolize service and friendship around the world. They connote action, for either the broad or narrow path is useless unless there are persons willing to travel it.

The complete text of the Outline of Policy of Rotary International in International Service appears on the following pages. . . .

Policy of Rotary International
in International Service

The Aim:

The aim of international service in Rotary is expressed in the fourth avenue of service, namely, to encourage and foster

The advancement of international understanding, good will and peace through a world fellowship of business and professional men united in the ideal of service.

The Rotary ideal of service finds expression only where there is liberty of the individual, freedom of thought, speech and assembly, freedom of worship, freedom from persecution and aggression and freedom from want and fear.

Freedom, justice, truth, sanctity of the pledged word and respect for human rights are inherent in Rotary principles and are also vital to the maintenance of international peace and order and to human progress.

Responsibility of the Individual Rotarian:

Each Rotarian is expected to make his individual contribution to the achievement of the ideal inherent in the fourth avenue of service.

Each Rotarian is expected to so order his daily personal life and business and professional activities that he will be a loyal and serving citizen of his own country.

Each Rotarian, wherever located, working as an individual, should help to create a well-informed public opinion. Such opinion will inevitably affect governmental policies concerned with the advancement of international understanding and good will toward all peoples.

As a world-minded Rotarian:

(a) He will look beyond national patriotism and consider himself as sharing responsibility for the advancement of international understanding, good will, and peace.

(b) He will resist any tendency to act in terms of national or racial superiority.

(c) He will seek and develop common grounds for agreement with peoples of other lands.

(d) He will defend the rule of law and order to preserve the liberty of

117

the individual so that he may enjoy freedom of thought, speech and assembly, freedom from persecution and aggression and freedom from want and fear.

(e) He will support action directed towards improving standards of living for all peoples, realizing that poverty anywhere endangers prosperity everywhere.

(f) He will uphold the principles of justice for mankind, recognizing that these are fundamental and must be world-wide.

(g) He will strive always to promote peace between nations and will be prepared to make personal sacrifices for that ideal.

(h) He will urge and practice a spirit of understanding of every other man's beliefs, as a step towards international good will recognizing that there are certain basic moral and spiritual standards which, if practiced, will insure a richer, fuller life.

Responsibility of the Rotary Club:

Rotary clubs should not engage in any corporate effort to influence governments, world affairs or international policies, but should devote their energies toward informing the individual Rotarian in these important matters, so that he will develop an enlightened and constructive attitude of mind.

A Rotary club may properly provide a forum for the presentation of public questions where such a course of action is designed to foster the fourth avenue of service. Where such questions are controversial, it is essential that both sides be adequately presented.

When international subjects are presented and discussed in a Rotary club, the speaker should be cautioned to avoid giving offense to peoples of other countries and it should be made clear that a Rotary club does not necessarily assume responsibility for opinions expressed by individual speakers at its meetings.

A Rotary club should not adopt resolutions of any kind dealing with specific plans relating to international affairs. It should not direct appeals for action from clubs in one country to clubs, peoples, or governments of another country or circulate speeches or proposed plans for the solution of specific international problems.

In all cases where international tensions develop between countries in which Rotary clubs exist, the utmost caution should be exercised by the clubs of the countries concerned and by clubs of other countries lest any action may increase ill will and misunderstanding.

Position of Rotary International:

R.I. consists of Rotary clubs located in many countries with many points of view. Therefore, no corporate action or corporate expression of opinion will be taken or given by R.I. on political subjects.